PHILOSOPHY AND CULTURE

Islam: A Semester Study

Barry Ferst, Ph.D.

CARROLL COLLEGE

Linus
Publications, Inc.

Published by Linus Publications, Inc.
Ronkonkoma, NY 11779

ISBN 10: 1-60797-226-3

ISBN 13: 978-1-60797-226-6

Printed in the United States of America.

This book is printed on acid-free paper.

Print Numbers 5   4   3   2   1

Table Of Contents

Preface...V

SECTION 1: LECTURES

Lecture One	Overview 3
Lecture Two	Islam: A Religion and a Way of Life 7
Lecture Three	Qur'an..13
Lecture Four	Mohammed...17
Graph A:	The Genesis of Sunni/Shi'ite Leadership 21
Lecture Five	A History of Islam: 570 to 1600 23
Graph B:	Family Relationships in the Rashidun 27
Lecture Six	A History of Islam: 1600 to 2011 33
Lecture Seven	Philosophy, Science, and Technology..........................43
Lecture Eight	Law and Jurisprudence 59
Lecture Nine	Prayer and Preaching 65

SECTION 2: SUPPORT MATERIALS

Timeline of Important Events 73

Fact Sheet Nation-States in *Dar al Islam* 79

Classifying Islamic Movements...82

Book Report List...84

Cinema Viewing List 87

Textbook . . . Readings List 91

Vocabulary 96

For Further Discussion: Technology..101

For Further Discussion: Decline in Philosophy and Science............................104

For Further Discussion: Martyrdom and Terrorism 109

For Further Discussion: Democracy and the Nation-State 113

For Further Discussion: Differences between Sunni and Shi'ite 115

For Further Discussion: Three Faiths 118

Readers' Circle Program 121

Resource Bibliography 124

Sample Test Questions 126

Question Response Worksheets 129

PREFACE

Islam: A Semester Study is designed to introduce college students to the Islamic faith and its expression in a variety of cultures around the world. In a semester course of approximately fifteen weekly, two-and-a-half hour sessions, participants would explore the most important features in Islam and would develop a sensitivity to cultures and communities that express the Islamic perspective. The goal is coming to understand the core of the Islamic tradition and the variations in the faith found in different Islamic communities.

Islam is one of three religions in the world that are rooted in the stories of Adam and Abraham. Because Islam is more than a religion (in the Western sense of that term) and is more accurately described as a way of living one's life, the material in this book will survey the history, practices, philosophy, and spirituality of this faith. Therefore, the contents of this book cross the traditional boundaries between philosophy, theology, and history and will address all three academic areas.

Because of the author's travels in the Middle East, the lands of the old Ottoman Empire, and North Africa, this textbook is slanted toward the Mediterranean Basin. Nevertheless, most of the lecture material remains true for other Muslim states, and those areas have been given consideration.

Of course a book cannot capture the rich life of the Muslim world. It follows that a semester of study must include videos, internet features, recorded music, and guest presentations by members of the faith. A Mediterranean meal would be appropriate, as would a musical performance, and a live reading of selections of Sufi poetry.

Each of the nine chapters in *Islam: A Semester Study* contains a sentence outline of important information regarding the chapter's topic. This material constitutes the core of the instructor's classroom lecture. Each chapter is followed by "Recall," a vocabulary of Arabic words and important terms found in that chapter; a "Reflect" section with suggestions for activities; and then a set of ten questions, "Respond," related to chapter information. The second half of the book has a variety of pedagogical support information. For example, there is a timeline of important events in Muslim history, a listing of fiction and nonfiction writings (novels, poetry, short story compilations) that make for entertaining and informative reading, a list of movies on DVD format from Muslim studios, and a tear-out section of "Reflect" question/ response sheets.

Several years of study would be required to gain a deep understanding of Islam. Such would be accomplished by majoring in Islamic studies, pursuing graduate education, and undergoing a period of cultural immersion. *Islam: A Semester Study* is designed to introduce college students who have enrolled in a semester course to gain an acquaintance with a fascinating and important culture different from their own.

SECTION 1
LECTURES

LECTURE 1

OVERVIEW

There are two reasons why a semester-long college course on Islam is so important at this time.

First, Americans need to gain an understanding of the rapidly growing number of their fellow citizens who are of the Islamic faith. And second, we need some insight into the culture of those countries in the Middle East to which the United States' foreign affairs are now so closely tied. (Of course, there is what might be called a perennial reason: Islam is a fascinating religion and way of life with an intriguing history.)

Here, then, is some basic information.

Islam is the religion of approximately one billion people worldwide. The founder was Mohammed, a businessman in Mecca, Arabia, who in A.D. 612 received a revelation from the angel Gabriel, ordering Mohammed to recite the words of Allah. Over the next twenty years, recitations poured from Mohammed and these became the Islamic Holy Scripture, the Qur'an (also, Koran). "Qur'an" means "recitation" in Arabic. The Qur'an is the eternal Word of Allah.

The birth of Islam is dated at 622—on the Islamic calendar, A.H.1 (*Anno Hijira*). It was in this year that Mohammed traveled to Medina, a caravan town north of Mecca, to gather willing followers. The trip is known as the *"hijira"* ("migration").

"Islam" literally means "submission," but implies "submission to the will of Allah." A Muslim ("true believer") is a follower of the Islamic faith. Many Muslims claim that the word "Islam" also finds its root in *"salam,"* Arabic for "peace."

Allah is the Supreme Being's name—just as English-speaking Christians call the Supreme Being, God. Allah has no Son, nor is there a Holy Spirit. Islam is a strict monotheism.

Muslims claim Abraham as their forefather through Hagar and Ishmael. Moses and Jesus are also great prophets, and Jews and Christians, like Muslims, are considered *ahl al kitab* (People of the Book). Mohammed is the final and greatest prophet.

With the death of Mohammed, the leadership of the faith was contested, and soon a split occurred which led to the two major divisions in Islam today—the Sunnis and the Shi'ites.

Islam spread very rapidly. Arab armies conquered the Middle East (much of the Byzantine-Christian Empire and all of the Sassanian-Zoroastrian Empire). Though most Arabs were Muslim, not all conquered nations were Arab, and not all conquered peoples immediately converted to Islam. There were Arabs (Arabia, most of modern Iraq), Persians (Iran), Syrians (roughly modern Syria, Jordan, Israel), Egyptians, Berbers (modern Tunisia, Algeria, Morocco), and Indians (northwestern India). By 750 most of Spain was under the control of Arab governors. By 1600 Islam had spread throughout Southeast Asia.

Islam spread in three ways—by peaceful conversion through the work of missionaries, by Muslim businessmen who set up trading outposts in non-Muslim countries, and by military force.

"Jihad" literally means "struggle" (or by implication, "struggle in the cause of Allah), and a Muslim faces three kinds of jihad. First, "jihad of the heart" means that I must struggle within myself to become a better true believer. Second, "jihad of the word" means I must struggle to spread my faith by preaching to others. Third, "jihad of the sword" means I must defend by all means available against anything that may threaten or attack Islam or its spread.

Islam is a religion, a political force, and a way of life. A Muslim is asked to do five things—the "Five Pillars of Islam". First, one must recite the creed, "There is no god but Allah, and Mohammed is his prophet." Second, give charity. Third, pray five times a day. Fourth, fast during certain periods of the year. Fifth, make the *hajj* (pilgrimage) to the holy city of Mecca to pray at the Kaaba (the holiest shrine in the Islamic world).

To one degree or another, nations which have a large population of Muslim citizens follow legal and moral codes, *sharia*, derived from the Qur'an, *hadith*, and *sunna* (the sayings and actions of Mohammed). Different Islamic states follow one of four different legal codes: Shafi, Hanabli, Maliki, and Hanafi. There is no formal hierarchy in the religious leadership of Islam, though in some forms of Islam the *iman* or *ayatollah* (literally "faith," but by extension "religious leader") has special status. A *fatwa* (a legal judgment) can be issued by any respected religious leader.

Turkey and Iraq have attempted to separate politics from faith while Saudi Arabia and the Taliban have attempted a strict Islamic government and society. Ruhollah Khomeini, both a spiritual and political dictator and both an *imam* and *ayatollah*, established the Islamic Republic of Iran, a Muslim theocracy. In contrast, "Ba'ath," Syria's dominant political party (and in Iraq, former president Saddam Hussein's party) means "Arab Socialist Resurrection"—nothing Islamic in this. Pakistan, a state largely populated with Sunni Muslims but proclaiming religious tolerance, unofficially suppresses Shi'ites and Christianity. With the largest Muslim population in the world (203 million out of 235 million citizens), Indonesia struggles to find the right path.

In December of 2010 protests against the government of Tunisia began what Western newscasters have called the "Arab Spring." Since that time various Arab states have seen people rising up to overthrow what protesters view as repressive governments. Tunisians succeeded in ousting Prime Minister Ghannouchi in January of 2011. Soon to follow were uprisings in Egypt, Yemen, Libya, Bahrain, Syria, and other Middle Eastern countries. For these countries, whether it will truly be an Arab Spring or more social repression and economic failure under a different set of dictators is yet to be determined.

The contemporary Middle East displays social and political problems that stem from at least three sources. First, there has been five centuries of disastrous leadership by sultans, amirs, ayatollahs, viziers, and caliphs. Second, there is the decay and final breakup of the Ottoman Empire in 1919 with England and France trying to divide up its remains among various tribes, clans, and families. And third, there are the effects of Western culture—liberalism, capitalism, representative democracy, science and technology, and pop culture--on the world.

Muslims are found in just about every nation. Most Muslims are not ethnic or cultural Arabs (Pakistan and Indonesia far and away have the largest populations of Muslims), but Arabic is the language of the Qur'an and Islamic tradition. Estimates of the number of people of the Islamic faith in the United States vary from five to seven million.

Recall:

ahl al kitab, ayatollah, hadith, hajj, hijira, imam, Islam, jihad, Muslim, Qur'an, salam, sharia, sunna

Reflect:

1. On Google Earth or www.googlemaps.com locate the countries listed in this chapter.

2. Draw up a timeline, showing a variety of important dates such as the death of Socrates, the birth of Jesus, the *hijira*, the Declaration of Independence, and some event from the present year.

Respond:

(See tear-out sheets at Question Response Worksheets at the end of this book.)

1. What reasons might be given for participating in a semester study of the Islamic faith?

2. As a young man, what was Mohammed's profession and what event changed his life?

3. What are the implications of the phrase "the Qur'an is the eternal Word of Allah" ?

4. Why is A.D. 622/A.H. 1 such an important date?

5. How did Islam spread?

6. What are the various meanings of the word "jihad"?

7. In what ways is Islam more than a religion?

8. What countries, in addition to Saudi Arabia, are mostly Muslim?

9. Contemporary Middle Eastern social and political problems stem from what two sources?

10. Which countries have the largest Muslim population?

LECTURE 2

ISLAM: A RELIGION AND A WAY OF LIFE

1. Islam, literally "submission," means by implication "submission to the will of Allah."

   - With the popular view that Islam and terrorism are inextricably associated, some scholars have asserted that the word is a derivative of *salam* (peace).

   - A Muslim (true believer) is a follower of the Islamic faith.

   - Until modern times, Europeans called Muslims "Mohammedans," thinking "Mohammedans are to Mohammed" as "Christians are to Christ."

   - The Qur'an (recitation) is the holy book of the Islamic faith.

   - Men and women should submit to the will of Allah and fear Him, for though He is separate from humankind, He provides guidance and determines the fate of all things.

   - Many scholars today call Islam, Christianity, and Judaism the three Abrahamic faiths.

   - Different terms are used to designate scholars who study Islam. An "Islamic scholar" would be a scholar who is a Muslim. "Orientalist" is a title used since the 19th century to classify scholars who study the Middle East (and may or may not be Muslim), though in recent years it has fallen into some disrepute. Recently there has been a move to replace "Orientalist" by "Islamicist," which is thought to be a more neutral title. Finally, an Islamist, may or may not be a scholar, but is a strong advocate, possibly in a radical way, for Islam.

2. Islam is not only a religion as one might think of Christianity as a religion, but also a way of life and a philosophy. The essence of Islam, if there is one, is found in the Five Pillars of Faith.

   - First, one must recite the *shahada* (creed): "*La illaha il-allah wa Mohammed ur-rasulillah*" ("There is no god but Allah, and Mohammed is his prophet"). Islam is a strict monotheism, and though it maintains that Ibrahim (Abraham), Musa (Moses), Isa (Jesus), and others was prophets, Mohammed is the prophet to the Arabs and the last prophet. Jews and Christians are "Peoples of the Book," meaning each was delivered of God's sacred word, and therefore these other faiths are to be respected. Yet, Jews and Christians perverted their scriptures and have fallen away from true and correct belief. As for polytheistic religions, these are simply bad.

- Second, everyone, unless in need of charity, must give *zakat* (charity). Moreover, it is no sin to be poor; rather, it is part of Allah's plan that some are made wealth and others poor. Muslim communities frequently support a *waqf* (literally "detention," but by implication, "to hold money back for an important cause")—a pious foundation whose monies can only be used for helping the poor, widows, and orphans. There are eight categories of people to whom charity is given:

    i.   the *fakir*—one who has neither means of a livelihood nor material possessions

    ii.   the *miskin*—one who cannot meet his basic needs

    iii.   the *amil*—workers who themselves collect and distribute charity

    iv.   the *muallafathul quloob*—one who converts to Islam

    v.   the *rigab*—one who wants to free himself from slavery

    vi.   the *gharmin*—one who is deeply in debt

    vii.   the *fisabillilah*—one who strives for the cause of Allah

    viii.   the *ibnus sabil*—one is stranded on a journey

- Third, Muslims are to do *salat* (pray) five times a day. Facing Mecca, they may pray in a building called a *mas'jid* (mosque), in a room of a house set aside for prayer only during times of prayer, or outdoors. Though it is best to pray in a group, one may pray alone. It may be that while traveling or when sick it is impossible to offer prayers, and so the obligation is removed.

- Fourth, one is to perform *sawm* (fasting) during Ramadan, a month of special religious significance. The fasting is conducted from dawn to sun set, and not even the drinking of water is allowed. Since Ramadan can come at different times during the year (given a lunar Muslim calendar) when the month is in the summer, the heat makes the fasting extremely difficult. Some Muslims may fast during certain other periods of the year.

- Fifth, one is to make the *hajj* (pilgrimage) to the holy city of Mecca to pray at the Kaaba, the holiest shrine in the Islamic world. Those who make the pilgrimage can add the title *hadji* to their names. Several rites and actions must be performed while on the *hajj*, including:

     i.   at *miqat* (specific places in Mecca where one vows to do the *hajj*) the pilgrim cleans himself/herself, and a male puts on the *ihram* (a special cloth clothing);

     ii.   the *talbiyah* (a special prayer) is said

     iii.   the *tawaaf* (circling the Kaaba) is completed

     iv.   the *istlam* (kissing or touching the black stone) is performed

     v.   the pilgrim leaves the Kaaba and goes to the Muqam-e-Ibrahim (Place of Abraham)

     vi.   the pilgrim goes to the field of Arafat

     vii. the pilgrim carries out the *Sa'ee* (running back and forth from Safa' to Marwah)

     viii. the pilgrim stones the pillars of Shatan (Satan)

3.   As Islam spread across the world certain adjustments by certain Muslims occurred to produce slight changes in the "Five Pillars."

- As Islam spread *adat/urf* (local customs/communal traditions) were blended into it, and some remained localized while others affected all of *Dar al Islam* (House of Islam).

- Examples of different custom-based practices include the following:

     i.   the practice of only three prayer sessions a day

     ii.   the assertion that there will be other prophets after Mohammed

     iii.   the extent to which women are to be covered

     iv.   prayer to deceased local holy men

4.   Islam contains an extensive code of ethical behavior. What constitutes ethical behavior is determined by the *ulamas'* (religious scholars) understanding of the Qur'an, along with the *sunna* and *hadith* (actions and non-Qur'anic sayings of Mohammed).

- As to what one should do, or *halal* (permitted), there are numerous maxims. For example, there are many specific directives (how to divide inheritance, how to contract a marriage), and general directives (kindness to strangers, giving alms).

- As to what one should not do, or *haram* (forbidden), there are (at least) seven sins that lead to Hell. These include:

     i.   the sin of *shirk* (an act of serious unrighteousness) such as practicing or advocating polytheism—a *kafir* (unbeliever)

     ii.   impiety

     iii.   sorcery

     iv.   unjust killing (murder and assassination)

     v.   flight from the battlefield (cowardice)

iv.   slandering a woman's honor

vii.   consuming the wealth of orphans and widows (greed).

- Muslims that go astray in their religious practices are called *fasiq* (impious, transgressor), but they are redeemable by repentance. However, one is allowed to practice *taqiyya* (dissimulation) if one is living under a corrupt regime. In order to survive, one must hide one's true beliefs.

5.   For many Muslims, there is no distinction between the sacred and the profane, the spiritual and the secular, the *regnum* and the *sacerdotum (royalty and church)*, or the private and the public spheres of life.

- Islam is a way to approach God, a rule book for private behavior and social interactions, and a guide to political and economic practices. Even the physical sciences are viewed within an Islamic framework.

- The Islamic faith does not have a formal hierarchy like the Catholic Church. Muslims come directly, with no intercessor, to Allah—He is always immediately present to the individual, and the phrase *inshallah* (God willing/if God so wills it) is frequently heard.

- A widely debated issue is whether or not Islam dictates a theocracy (rule by God; alternately, rule by a religion's religious leadership and God's laws as revealed in a holy scripture).

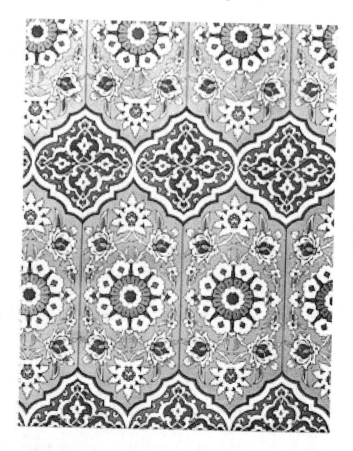

Recall:

adat/urf, Dar al Islam, fasiq, halah, haram, inshallah, Islamist, Islamicist, kafir, mas'jid, Orientalist, regnum and sacerdotum, salat, sawm, shahada, shirk, taqiyya, ulama, waqf, zakat

Reflect:

From the web browser go to www.youtube.com and search for the word "*shahada*". Review several of the entries you find for this word.

Respond:

1. What do Muslims believe about Allah?
2. In what fashion have Christians misunderstood the naming of the Islamic faith?
3. What is the Qur'an?
4. What are the five core beliefs that unite all Muslims?
5. How has *adat* affected the practices of Muslims?
6. What is Islam's view of other religions?
7. What sorts of things are viewed as sinful?
8. Who are these figures: Ibrahim, Musa, Nuh, Isa, Ishaaq?
9. What distinctions can be made between the Qur'an, hadith, and sunna?
10. How do Muslims view the different aspects of their daily life and more generally "reality"?

QUR'AN

1.   The Qur'an (also Koran) is the sacred scripture to those people of the Islamic faith. It is the word of Allah, and it is not a created object, but the eternal word of Allah.

  •   The proof the Qur'an is from Allah is its supernatural beauty. The Qur'an itself says this.

  •   Muslims see the Qur'an as Allah's final revelation to humankind.

  •   The Qur'an must always be written in Arabic.

  •   Whether the Qur'an is or is not a creation was an important philosophical and theological debate during the early years of the faith.. In many ways the debate parallels early Christian arguments concerning whether Jesus was created or begotten.

2.   The word *"qur'an"* means "recitation." Tradition holds that over twenty-three years from 610 to 632 the angel Jibril (Gabriel) visited the Prophet Mohammed and told Mohammed to recite the words of Allah. Scribes took down the recited *sura*s (chapters).

  •   However, a second, less popular tradition holds that the 27ᵗʰ day of Ramadan is the day when the Qur'an as a whole came to be delivered to Mohammed. (To make the two claims coherent, it is said that Mohammad was first told by Gabriel about the forthcoming Qur'an on this date, or a similar interpretation.)

  •   There are 114 *sura* (chapters) and about 6,200 *ayat* (verses) in Qur'an. Scholars are not in full agreement on the number of verses: some view the Qur'an as having only 6,000 *ayat*, while others list as many as 6,236 (the most widely cited number).

  •   The Qur'an's present structure is thought to be based on what Islamic tradition claims as the Uthmanic codex of c. 650. Nevertheless, some scholars maintain that the Qur'an was not in its present form until two or three hundred years later.

  •   Some passages in the Qur'an are similar to passages in the Bible. Mohammed's recitation alludes to the *Injil* (Gospels) from which is adopted and adjusted God's selection of Mary.

- Even of greater interest, Mohammed recites stories that are not in the canon, but are in other gospels.

3. Some scholars contend that the verses which deal with general moral and metaphysical principles were the earliest delivered verses, while verses that deal with practical issues of a new community of believers came later. In the Qur'an as it now exists, shorter verses come first, and longer verses are placed later in the book.

    - Chapters are referred to by scholars as either Meccan or Medinan, depending on where they are thought to be delivered.

    - Each *sura* except the ninth begins with the *Bismillah*, "In the name of God, most gracious, most merciful . . . ."

4. Much in the Qur'an appears to be moral directives phrased as reminders as to what is the proper behavior. It is as though people know the right thing to do, but they need to be reminded of it.

    - Some of this fits the traditional "wisdom literature" of *Works and Days* and inter-testamental biblical writings.

    - A certain oracular style is apparent throughout the *suras*.

    - From the phrasings in the *sura,* it is apparent that the various messages are addressed to men (for example, comments on women).

    - From *sura* two of the Qur'an, *al-Baqara*, The Cow. Charity: 2:215, 2:270, 2:271. Gambling and drinking: 2:219. War: 2:216, 2:217, 2:244; Women (marriage) 2:221; Women (sexual intercourse) 2:223.

    - Certain verses came to Mohammed as justifications of actions he was about to take or had just taken.

5. Yet the Qur'an provides more than moral directives. It provides pictures of a well-lived life, a well-organized and regulated society, and the structure of the universe.

    - Some scholars suggest that all scientific knowledge and discovery (at least the roots thereof) are contained in the pages of the Qur'an.

    - The same holds true for social intercourse and civic organization.

6. Though Muslim theologians say that the meaning of the Qur'an is clear, historically such "clarity" has depended on *tafsir* (scholarly writings meant to clarify and illuminate various verses).

    - One *tafsir* issue is the need to explain Qur'anic verses to people who would not know the original setting of the deliverance of a verse, but need to know it to fully understand its meaning.

    - A second *tafsir* issue has to do with verses that came later in the period of revelation that appear to contradict or cancel out earlier verses. This is known as *nasik* (abrogation).

    - Another *tafsir* issue is verses that could be read in two ways. Does Islam accept all religions, only monotheist religions, or reject all others?

- Mystics in the Muslim tradition, *sufi/darwesh/fakir*, claim a deeper, hidden and secret meaning to Qur'anic words, reading them as symbols of a supernatural sort.

7. Various tools can be used to come to an understanding and proper application of the Qur'an. These tools include:

   i. *Ijtihad*—interpretation and reinterpretation of passages by Islamic scholars

   ii. *ijma* (consensus); *ijma al-aimmah* (consensus of the leaders)—Scholars attempt to reach a broad consensus on the correct way to understand a passage

   iii. *taqlid*—Scholars follow in a tradition set out by earlier scholars

8. Muslims have differing opinions as to how the Qur'an is to be read, interpreted, and applied. Some Muslims are wary of *bid'at* (unwarranted innovation in applying various Islamic principles to life). Conservative Muslims believe innovation to be a bad thing. Nevertheless, in the light of modern science, democratic movements, and Western culture, interpretation seems to be called for.

Recall:

ayat, bid'at, Bismillah, ijtihad, ijma, nasik, sura, sufi, darwesh, fakir, tafsir, taqlid

Reflect:

On the internet or at a library go to the Qur'an's second *sura*, The Cow, and find as many references as you are able to Mary and Jesus.

Respond:

1. Can you describe what Qur'anic recitation sounds like to you?
2. The proof that the Qur'an is from Allah is its supernatural beauty. The Qur'an itself says this. What can be said about this proof?
3. What insights can be gained by comparing the Qur'an to the Bible?
4. Can Mohammed recite *suras* which at the same time are Allah's *very* words?
5. Islamicists wonder if much pre-Islamic material—ethical codes and ideas about divinity—got adopted into the Qur'an. Could you cite some?
6. Consider issues surrounding *ijtihad*. When do we have a valid interpretation of something, and is there anything that can be understood without interpretation?
7. Some claim that the Qur'an is also a book of scientific explanations about physical reality. How would this be justified?
8. Why do think the *Bismillah* is important?
9. What Christian or Jewish parallels are there to *tafsir*?
10. Why is it important that a "real" Quran be in Arabic?

LECTURE 4

MOHAMMED

1. The earliest biography of Mohammed, *Life of the Messenger of God*, was composed c. 760 in Baghdad by Ibn Ishaq (704-767). Though this book is lost, there does exist a revised edition of this work by Ibn Hisham (d. 833), *The Life of the Prophet*.

    *   Ibn Ishaq's book appears to have cast Mohammad's life as paralleling a number of biblical and Gospel narratives. For example, in a parallel to the Gospel story of loaves and fishes, when Mohammed is with some of his closest followers, he is able to miraculously provide more than enough meat and drink from the little that was originally set before them.

    *   According to Muslims, Mohammed's coming was foretold in Christian scriptures. For example, Muslim authors cite the Gospel of John at 16:7-15.

2. Mohammed was born c. 570 in Mecca, a few weeks after his father 'Abdullah died, and as was Arab custom, his grandfather, Abd Al' Muttalib, sent him to live in the Arabian desert with a Bedouin foster-mother.

    *   After a few years he was returned to his mother, Aminah, but she died when Mohammed was eight. He then was taken in by his uncle, his father's brother, Abu-Talib.

    *   Abu-Talib was not well-off, and so Mohammed first worked as a shepherd, and then at ten, he worked with his uncle on a caravan to Syria. One story has it that at twelve while on a caravan trip, Bahira, a monk, identified Mohammed as the Messenger of Allah. Bahira pointed to a birthmark on Mohammed's shoulder as the Seal of Prophethood.

    *   Islam traces Mohammed's lineage back through forty generations to Ishmael first born of Ibrahim and then to Adam.

    *   He belonged to the Banu Hashim (Hashimites), a minor clan in the important Quraysh tribe.

3. As a young man, Mohammed already had a reputation for honesty and integrity, and he came to direct a successful caravan business for a rich Meccan widow, Khadija bint Ishaq (c. 555-619).

- He married Khadija when he was twenty-five and she was, some say twenty-eight, others forty. The happy marriage produced five (or six?) children.

- Khadija died at fifty-one (or sixty-four), and afterwards Mohammed took several wives (eleven to fourteen) his favorite being Aisha. Including the offspring he had with Khadija, he had four daughters and three sons, but only Fatimah survived childhood.

- Nine of Mohammed's wives were from the Quraysh (this includes Khadija). Two or three were from the Jewish tribes of Medina. One was Mary the Copt (Christian) a gift from an Egyptian tribal leader.

- Only Mohammed was allowed this many wives—others could have only four, though throughout history some have had many wives kept in a harem.

4. Mecca was not only a caravan city, but also the Arabian center of polytheistic idol worship. Surrounding the Kaaba were 360 (or 350) idols, though it does not appear hat Mohammad was ever an idol-worshipper or a polytheist.

   - In 605 the Kaaba was destroyed by fire, and as the legend goes Mohammed was appointed by Meccans, because of trustworthiness, to select the proper spot in the rebuilt Kaaba's walls to place the black stone.

   - Therefore, 605 is cited as the year that Mohammed became more absorbed in spiritual undertakings.

   - The period before Mohammed's birth is called the age of *jahiliya* (confusion, or by implication, the polytheistic helter-skelter world before Mohammed's revelations). However, the Qur'an makes reference to Adam, Abraham, Moses, Mary, and Jesus.

5. In 610, at 40 years of age, toward the end of Mohammed's fifth Ramadan retreat, he was visited by Gabriel, who told him that Allah (literally, "the God", al-the, lah-god) had chosen him as his messenger to bring Arabs monotheism and the principles for a morally upstanding life.

   - When Gabriel first approached Mohammed, he was meditating in the Cave of Hira just outside Mecca. Gabriel told Mohammed to recite the words of Allah, and Mohammed said he could not. Gabriel then demanded that Mohammed do this and forced him to recite.

   - Mohammed began to recite the words of Allah, the first said to be: "In the name of God, the Most Merciful, the All-Merciful. Recite, with the name of thy Lord Who created, Created man from what clings; Recite, and they Lord the Most Bounteous, Who taught by the pen, Taught man what he knew not." This became Qur'an 96:1-5.

   - Mohammed was initially frightened, thinking that *Shatan* (Satan) or a *jinn* (a mischievous genie) might have been behind this; but Khadija reassured him, saying, have faith and to take this occurrence as a revelation from Allah.

- It was three years (some say one) before Mohammed received more divine revelations, and in these various religious, moral, and social principles came forth such as the directive of worshipping only one god; that caring for orphans, widows, and the destitute was a moral obligation; and that drinking alcoholic beverages and gambling were forbidden social practices.

- The Qur'an was not revealed all at once, but over twenty-three years as responses to events in Mohammed's life and the growing community of Muslims.

- This is the Islamic Golden Age and prophetic period.

6.   At first Mohammed preached secretly to friends and relatives, but soon afterwards he began to speak publicly. His message focused on three key principles:

i.   One transcendent god (and hence the denunciation of polytheism and idol worship).

ii.   Resurrection of the dead.

iii. The Last Judgment.

- As if to prove the claim of being God's prophet, one night Mohammed was taken from the nearest temple (the Kaaba?) to the furthest temple (Jerusalem's Temple Mount?) and then flown on the back of a magical horse, Barag (Baraq/Barak) to the seventh heaven where Mohammed communed with Allah. This journey (which possibly is a combination of two distinct stories) is called the *mi'raj* (ascension), and it may be referring to in sura 17:1, the "Night Journey."

- Though initially Mohammad and his followers prayed toward Jerusalem, in 624 the *qiblah* (prayer direction) was changed to point toward Mecca.

7.   There was a great deal of resistance to Mohammed's message in polytheist Mecca, and because Mohammed was attacking Meccan religious tradition, the Meccan leadership (the powerful "clans" within the Quraysh tribe) turned on Mohammed. His uncle Abu Talib who had much prestige in Mecca defended him as did Khadija, but they both died in 619, and knowing that leaders of the Quraysh would try to kill him, he decided it would be best to leave Mecca.

- 622 C.E./A.H.1 is the date of "the breaking of old ties," the *hijira*, when Mohammed traveled from Mecca to Yatrib (a caravan city approximately 250 miles to the north, and soon to be called Medina— the "city" of Mohammad).

- The *hijira* marks the foundation date of the faith—A.H.1—and the date for counting up the years and centuries on the Muslim calendar (*anno hijira*, year of the *hijira*).

- In Medina Mohammed found Jewish and Christian tribes fighting each other and they appointed him as their peacemaker. He fashioned an alliance between the Christian, Jewish, and Muslim peoples in Medina.

- The *ashab* (companions of the Prophet) are his followers who left Mecca for Medina.

- The *ansar* (helpers) are the first Medinans to join with Mohammed. This designation, like the *ashab* designation, had political significance in the formation of early Islamic governance.

8. Over the next eight years there were *ghazi* (raids, or raiding parties; sing. *ghazwa*) conducted by Mohammed and his followers on the Meccan camel caravans to capture booty. Small-scale wars were carried out between the Meccans and Medinans, until in 630, Mohammed was victorious and the Meccans surrendered their city to Mohammed.

   - Two famous battles were the Battle of Badr (624) and the Battle of Uhud (625), and though the outcomes of both were inconclusive, the Battle of Uhud in many ways was actually a defeat as many Muslims were killed. A third battle, the Battle of the Trench (627) was a stand-off. Nevertheless, the Muslim community was growing in size and its military forces continually were gaining in strength.

   - The concept of raiding parties rather than full-scale warfare will remain a tradition in Muslim history into the modern period.

   - Many Arab tribes joined together under Mohammed's leadership.

   - In 629 Mohammed sent a letter to neighboring Eastern Roman Orthodox Christian Empire Byzantine Emperor Heraclius (575-641) to join him in the Muslim faith.

9. Finally, in 630 Mohammed was able to return to Mecca, and the Meccan leadership, seeing the overwhelming power of the Muslims, capitulated to Mohammad. Some historians write that Mohammed seized Mecca with an army of 10,000 though no blood was shed. The Meccans promptly converted to Islam.

   - With Mohammed's final victory, the Kaaba, the ancient square block temple in the center of Mecca, was cleared of idols and was reconstituted as the center of the Islamic faith.

   - Soon, various Arabian tribes either converted to Islam or came under the sway of Islamic power. Some of these conversions or acceptance of Islamic power came peacefully, at other times by force.

   - It remains an important historical question as to why the Meccans so easily accepted Islam.

10. In 632 Mohammed (63 years old) died in Medina after performing the Hajj to Mecca.

    - He left behind Islam, the third great Abrahamic religion, and a way of living one's life as a Muslim.

- He unified the tribes of Arabia and provided both an ideology and a faith that would soon carry Islam west across North Africa to the Atlantic and east to northern India.

- He is viewed by most Muslims as "the perfect man" and his life as reported in the *sunna* (along with the Qur'an) fashions Islamic behavior.

- The most important proof of his prophethood was his selection by Allah to be the deliverer of the Qur'an.

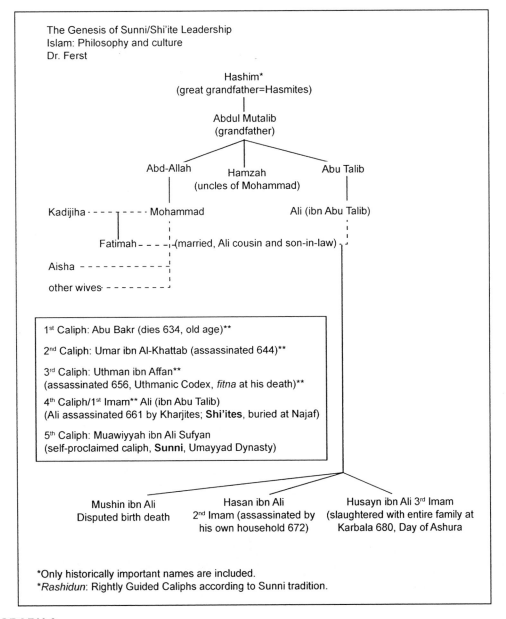

The Genesis of Sunni/Shi'ite Leadership
Islam: Philosophy and culture
Dr. Ferst

Hashim*
(great grandfather=Hasmites)

Abdul Mutalib
(grandfather)

Abd-Allah   Hamzah   Abu Talib
(uncles of Mohammad)

Kadijiha - - - - - - - Mohammad   Ali (ibn Abu Talib)

Fatimah - - - - (married, Ali cousin and son-in-law)

Aisha - - - - - - - - - - -

other wives - - - - - - - -

1st Caliph: Abu Bakr (dies 634, old age)**

2nd Caliph: Umar ibn Al-Khattab (assassinated 644)**

3rd Caliph: Uthman ibn Affan**
(assassinated 656, Uthmanic Codex, *fitna* at his death)**

4th Caliph/1st Imam** Ali (ibn Abu Talib)
(Ali assassinated 661 by Kharjites; **Shi'ites**, buried at Najaf)

5th Caliph: Muawiyyah ibn Ali Sufyan
(self-proclaimed caliph, **Sunni**, Umayyad Dynasty)

Mushin ibn Ali   Hasan ibn Ali   Husayn ibn Ali 3rd Imam
Disputed birth death   2nd Imam (assassinated by   (slaughtered with entire family at
                            his own household 672)   Karbala 680, Day of Ashura

*Only historically important names are included.
*Rashidun: Rightly Guided Caliphs according to Sunni tradition.

GRAPH A

Recall:

Allah, ansar, ashab, bint, ghazi, hubal, jahiliya, jinn, mi'raj, qiblah, Shatan

Reflect:

Make a listing of the ways in which the story of Jesus is different from the story of Mohammed.

Respond:

1.   Describe Mohammed's childhood years.
2.   As a young man, what profession did Mohammed take up?
3.   What sorts of spiritual activities did Mohammed participate in before his first revelation?
4.   How did Mohammad respond to Gabriel's commands?
5.   How did the Meccans respond to Mohammed?
6.   What occurred in 622?
7.   Why would Muslims make a distinction between the ashab and the ansar?
8.   What transpired in the eight years between Mohammed's sojourn in Medina and his return to Mecca?
9.   What was Mohammed's immediate legacy?
10. What is the cultural force of seeing Mohammed as "the perfect man"?

A HISTORY OF ISLAM: 570 to 1600

1. To understand the history of Islam, Europeans and Americans must set aside their views of history and see the flow of centuries from the Muslim perspective from which a very different understanding of the past and present emerges.

    - Europeans and Americans view history from the perspective of important events in Western history.

        Egypt and the Hebrew Peoples (2000 to 500 B.C.E.)

        The Classical Age of the Greeks and the Romans (500 B.C.E to 500)

        Jesus and the Early Years of Christianity

        The European Dark Ages and Middle Ages (500 to 1350)

        The Renaissance (1350 to 1600)

        Columbus and the European Discovery of the Western Hemisphere

        The Age of Reason and the Enlightenment (1600 to 1850)

        The Discovery of the Three Laws of Motion by Isaac Newton

        The Birth of Representative Democracies

        The Industrial Revolution

        The Contemporary World (1850 to the present)

        The Cosmology of Albert Einstein

        The Atomic Age, Information Age, Post Modernism

        Popular culture and the Power of the Middle Class

    - However, the Muslim perspective frames history in a very different fashion.

        The Biblical World of Adam, Ibrahim/Abraham, Ishmael, Musa/Moses, and Isa/Jesus

The Age of *Jahiliya*

Mohammed and the Rise of Islam (570)

The *Rashidun* (first four caliphs)

The Classical Golden Age of Islam (1 A.H./622 to 1300)

The Mongol Invasions (1250-1450)

Safavid, Mughal, and Ottoman Empires (1400 to 1920)

Social and Political Stagnation

Western colonialism

The Breakup of Safavid, Mughal, and Ottoman Empires

Western Political Dominance

Dar al Islam Divided on the Model of Western States (1919 to 1948)

Secularism, Salafiism, Terrorism

Arab Spring

2.   The Islamic faith was born in the Arabian Peninsula, a sandy and barren place, sparsely populated by Bedouin tribes, with a few oasis towns such as Mecca and Yatrib (Medina) on the camel caravan routes.

- One major route traversed by long caravans of camels carrying spices and incense was from the southern tip of Arabia due north to Syria and the Mediterranean coast.

- The city of Mecca later grew up around the well (the well of Zamzam) where Hagar and Ishmael came when sent away by Abraham at Sarah's urging.

- The Hijaz (literally "the barrier") is the western coastal area of Arabia bordering the Red Sea and containing the cities of Jeddah, Mecca and Medina.

3.   To the northwest of Arabia was the Byzantine Empire (modern Turkey, Syria-west, Lebanon, Israel, Greece, and the Balkans), and to the northeast was the Sassanian Empire (modern Syria-east, Iraq, Iran, Jordan). These two empires were constantly at war with each other.

- "Byzantine Empire" is a name given by historians to the Eastern Roman Empire as it existed from 350 to 1453. Nevertheless, the "Byzantines" never referred to themselves as such—they were Romans with their capital being Constantinople (the city of Constantine the Great, or rather New Rome).

- The Byzantines and the Sassanians were in constant warfare where their fluid borders met. To the south, the Arabs were never seen as a threat.

4.   Traditionally, the founding date given for Islam is 622 A.D. (A.H. 1), the year that Mohammed left Mecca for Medina with a small group of followers.

- However, many Muslims will say that Islam really started with the first true believer in the one god, Allah, and that believer was Abraham. Abraham's first born was Ishmael (the important son), and it was Ishmael that Allah called on Abraham to sacrifice.

5. Mohammed died in 632, and after much argument Abu Bakr was appointed *khalifah* (alternately, *khalifah*, literally "deputy," but by implication "leader of the faithful") over the *umma* (community of believers). Wars of *riddah* (apostasy) broke out as tribes broke away from the leadership of Abu Bakr. Abu Bakr successfully reunited the tribes, but he died within two years of assuming the *caliphat*, and Umar ibn al-Khattab took over the leadership of the *umma*. However, *caliph* Umar was assassinated in 644, and Uthman ibn Affan became the third *caliph*.

  - It was Abu Bakr who determined that apostasy (rejection of one's religion) was to be viewed as treason to the *umma*. Treason was punishable by death and for many today, this principle still holds. Religion and politics, therefore, are inextricably linked.

  - When Mohammed first began to spread the faith Umar ibn al-Khattab was an enemy, but one day Umar came across his sister reading the Qur'an, and he snatched it away and read the *sura* called Ta Ha that she was reading. The power of the verses immediately caused him to drop his hatred and become a Muslim.

  - There is the suggestion that Umar was the first to use the Arabic word *"jihad,"* not as "striving" but as "fighting." This occurred when he was at war with the Sassanian Empire. Closely tied to this understanding of jihad is that the world is divided into two and only two realms: *Dar al Islam* and *Dar al Harb (house/land of war)*.

  - The Qur'an in its present form was fashioned by Caliph Uthman's scholars c. 650. The work is known as the "Uthmanic codex." Uthman also fashioned the Muslim calendar, using the *hijira* as year 1.

6. Rapidly, Islamic armies captured the island of Cyprus, much of North Africa, Iran, Afghanistan, and northwest India (the Sind).

  - Armies under the banner of Islam invaded Egypt, Syria, and Iraq. They took Jerusalem and easily defeated the Sassanians and the Byzantines. In 637 the Sassanian capital, Ctesiphon, fell to the Muslims and by 642 the victory over the Sassanians was complete.

  - Initially, Arabs did not ask or demand conquered people to convert to Islam. One reason for this was that the much needed *jizra* (taxes on non-Muslims) could be extracted.

  - Though many people tend to equate Arab with Muslim and vice versa, this equation is correct only prior to the Muslim conquests. *Dar al Islam* is made up of Arabs, Egyptians, Persians, Indians, and many other ethnic groups.

- The early Muslim world was not one of equality. Full-blooded Arab Muslims were on top; next were Muslims with one Arab and one non-Arab parent; next down were non-Arab Muslims; then non-Arab Muslims whose parents were not Muslims; then non-Muslims who were Peoples of the Book; finally polytheists.

7. Uthman was assassinated in 656 and Muslims split between the leadership of Ali ibn Abi Talib and Muawiyyah ibn Ali Sufyan.

- Relationships among early Muslim leadership:

--Mohammed is from clan Banu Hashim and tribe Quraysh. He marries Aisha whose father is Abu Bakr (first caliph).

--Umar ibn al-Khattab (second caliph) is from Banu Adi clan of the Quraysh. His cousin was Muawiyyah ibn Abu/Ali Sufyan, and he appointed him governor of Damascus.

--Uthman's (third caliph) uncle and aunt are Abu Sufyan and his wife Hind, both members of the Quraysh tribe, clan Banu Umayyad.

--Ali ibn Abu Talib (fourth caliph) was the cousin of Mohammed and son-in-law through his marriage to Mohammed's daughter, Fatima.

--Muawiyyah ibn Abu/Ali Sufyan's (challenger to Ali) parents were Abu Sufyan and his wife Hind. Aisha politically supported Muawiyyah.)

Family Relationships in the *Reshidun*

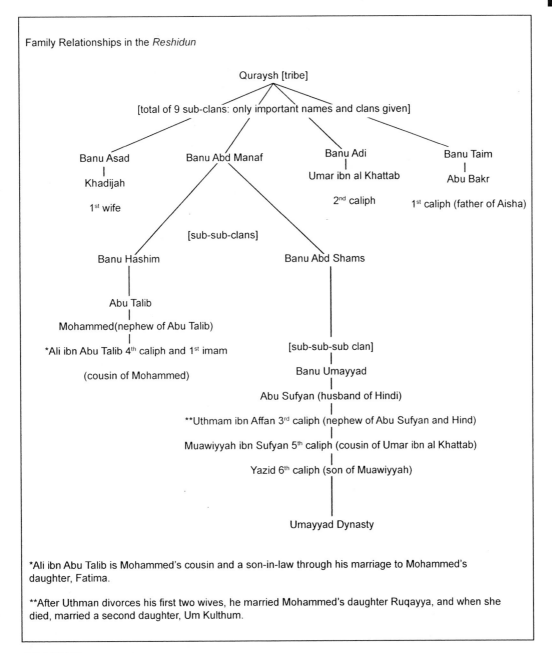

Quraysh [tribe]

[total of 9 sub-clans: only important names and clans given]

Banu Asad
|
Khadijah

1st wife

Banu Abd Manaf

Banu Adi
|
Umar ibn al Khattab

2nd caliph

Banu Taim
|
Abu Bakr

1st caliph (father of Aisha)

[sub-sub-clans]

Banu Hashim

Abu Talib
|
Mohammed(nephew of Abu Talib)
|
*Ali ibn Abu Talib 4th caliph and 1st imam

(cousin of Mohammed)

Banu Abd Shams

[sub-sub-sub clan]

Banu Umayyad
|
Abu Sufyan (husband of Hindi)
|
**Uthmam ibn Affan 3rd caliph (nephew of Abu Sufyan and Hind)
|
Muawiyyah ibn Sufyan 5th caliph (cousin of Umar ibn al Khattab)
|
Yazid 6th caliph (son of Muawiyyah)

Umayyad Dynasty

*Ali ibn Abu Talib is Mohammed's cousin and a son-in-law through his marriage to Mohammed's daughter, Fatima.

**After Uthman divorces his first two wives, he married Mohammed's daughter Ruqayya, and when she died, married a second daughter, Um Kulthum.

GRAPH B

- The four caliphs (Ali ibn Abi Talib is the fourth) that follow Mohammed from the period of 632 to 661 are known as the *Rashidun* (the rightly guided apostles/ones/deputies).

- Modern *salafiists* (Muslims who believe that the period of the first four caliphs was a time of pure and ideal Islam) want to return to what they see as a Golden Age.

8. With the hostile split between Muawiyyah and Ali, the *umma* was in a state of *fitnah* (disorder or heresy) as civil war broke out. Ali was assassinated in 661, and the Shiah i-Ali (the followers of Ali) soon came to see themselves as the Shi'ite sect of Islam, while the followers of Muawiyyah became the Sunni sect. Muawiyyah founded the Umayyad dynasty with Damascus (not Mecca) as its capital.

    *   Ali was assassinated in 661 by a member of a Muslim splinter sect, the Kharijites, who were unhappy that Ali appeared to compromise with Muawiyyah.

    *   At Muawiyyah's death, his son, Yazid I (645 to 683), was proclaimed the next (Umayyad) caliph. Husayn ibn Ali would not swear allegiance to Yazid I, and at Karbala in 680, Husayn and his entire family and associates were killed. Shi'ites today mourn that event and see him as the first Shi'ite *imam*.

    *   In 683 the Kaaba in Mecca was destroyed by fire during a civil war between those for or against Yazid I.

9. From 660 to 750 the Umayyads led the Sunni Islamic nation.

    *   In 691 the Umayyad caliph, Abd al-Malik built the Dome of the Rock in Jerusalem, but the reason for its construction remains in question.

    *   Muslims crossed the straits of Gibraltar in 712. Most of Spain soon became part of *Dar al Islam*. Their advance was stopped by the Christian Charles Martel at the Battle of Poitiers (France) in 732.

    *   Imam Abu Hanifah (699 to 767) was the first Muslim to attempt to create an organized *fiqh* (body of religious law and jurisprudence). Ultimately, Islamic scholars developed four *madhab*s (schools of law and jurisprudence).

10. In 749 the Umayyad dynasty was overthrown and the Abbasids came to power. During the centuries of the Abbasid dynasty, the peoples of *Dar al Islam* developed new agricultural and irrigation techniques, studied and expanded Greek philosophy, advanced Greco-Roman medicine and astronomy, and adopted Byzantine and Persian aesthetic sensibilities.

    *   Caliph Ma'mun (c. 820) had a dream in which Aristotle appeared and told him to study the works of the Greek philosophers. Ma'mun understood his dream to mean that he should aid in any way he could the study of Greco-Roman philosophy and science. In 833 he founded the *Bayt al Hikma* (House of Science) in Baghdad.

    *   Under the caliphate of Harun al-Rashd, a great cultural flowering occurred in the arts and sciences. Al Kindi (805-873) is thought of as the first Islamic philosopher. Al Farabi (870-950) is known as the "Father of Islamic Neo-Platonism."

    *   Al-Rashd promoted the study of *fiqh* (religious law). His scholars separated out trustworthy *hadith* (sayings of Mohammed) from less-

than-completely trustworthy and not-at all trustworthy *hadith*. All of this led to a coherent formation of *Shari'a* ("path" or "way," and by implication, general and universal sacred Islamic law).

11. Over the next several centuries, *Dar al Islam* split into various "states" under a variety of *sultans* and dynasties. Though the Abassid dynasty continued, real political power devolved to the Samanids (Sunni Iranian dynasty), the Hamdanids (greater Syria), the Buyids (Baghdad, southern Iraq, Oman), Ikshids (Egypt, Syria, Hijaz), Shi'ite Fatimids (Tunisia, Egypt, parts of greater Syria), the Ghaznavids (northern India), Seljuk Turks (central and western Asia), etc.

- The great cultural flowering of Islam continued. Baghdad and Cordoba became important cultural centers.

- Firdausi (940-1020) wrote the *Shahnama* (*Book of Kings*) an epic history of Persia from the beginning of the world till the arrival of Islam.

- Known in the West as Avicenna (980-1037), Ibn Sina displayed his great abilities with *falsafah* (philosophy).

- Sufi mystical traditions began. Abu Hamid al-Ghazzali (1058-1111), a highly respected Muslim theologian in the Ash'arite tradition rejected the "rationality" of the philosophers.

- Known in the West as Averroes, the Spanish-Arab philosopher, physician and jurist of *Shari'a*, Abu al-Wlid ibn Ahmad ibn Rushd (1126-1198), was working at absorbing Aristotle's philosophy into Islam. He attempted to undo Al-Ghazzali's position, but failed.

12. In Europe the *Reconquista* (the conquest of Spain by Christians) began around 1000.

- Spain's Muslim rulers accommodated both Christians and Jews in a multi-faith society.

- Muslim Spain had developed a wealthy and sophisticated "high" culture.

- Catholic theologian-philosophers had access to long lost Greek and Roman literature, science, and philosophy as Arabic books were translated into Latin by scholars in Cordoba and Toledo.

13. In Asia Minor in 1071 the Seljuk Turks defeated Byzantine armies in the Battle of Manzikurt. Soon the Seljuk Turks led by Alp Arslan ("Heroic Lion," 1029-1072) controlled most of Turkey.

- Malik Shah, Alp Arslan's son, assumed power after his father's death, but he had to confront an opponent in his own ranks, Hassan Sabbah, founder of the Cult of Assassins.

- The Assassins undermined both Sunni and Shi'ite power by developing a corps of *fedayeen* (sacrificers) to assassinate political leaders. The fedayeen knew that they would be captured and killed by the followers of those they had killed.

14. In response to his loss of much of his empire, Byzantine Emperor Alexius Commenus I appealed to Western Europe's Christians to help fight the Seljuks.

- Commenus' appeal brought Pope Urban II to announce the First Crusade. In 1099 the Crusaders took Jerusalem and a great slaughter of Jews and Moslems ensued.

- In 1187 Saladin defeated the Crusaders and re-captured Jerusalem. The Franj (what Muslims called the Crusaders) held on to their small principalities through a network of impregnable fortresses for approximately 150 years.

- Though at the time the Franj/European/Christian Crusades were seen by Muslims as a minor irritant, today they are cited as a symbol of the West's interests in the Middle East.

15. The 13th and 14th centuries saw the great and terrifying invasions of the Mongols into Islamic Asia. Many Muslim cities were destroyed—in 1258 Baghdad burned and in 1260 Aleppo fell.

- The first invasions into Muslim lands were led by Genghis Khan (1162-1227) in 1226.

- Ultimately, the Mongols converted to Islam.

- On the heels of the Mongols, came a second Turkic people (Ottoman Turks rather than Seljuk Turks).

- In northern India the Mongols formed the Mughal Empire.

- Such difficult and disastrous events brought forth Muslim thinkers who saw in the horror Allah's punishment of those who had gone astray. Ibn Taymiyyah (1263-1328) was one such philosopher-theologian who called for Muslims to return to a proper (and stricter) form of Muslim life.

16. By the 14th century *Dar al Islam* was facing a severe cultural decline. No single factor was responsible, even considering the havoc caused by the Mongol invasions.

- Warfare: Continuous warfare devastated lands and armies, not only with the Mongol invasions and the Turks, but among competing sultans, mullahs, and imams.

- Intellectual production: Ibn Nadim, author of *Kitab al Fihrist*, (a 10th century index of Arab literature), reported that in the 9th century 1,416 secular works were produced in Islamic lands; however, by the 14th century the number had dropped to 305. Nevertheless, it wasn't only the number of scholarly writings that decreased; what was produced was of inferior intellectual quality. *Za'iraja* (astrology) was considered an important science, but by the 12th century the astronomical observations that served astrology had been degraded into worthless mystical charts.

- Philosophical speculation: The 14th century observer of Islamic culture, Ibn Khaldun, maintained that philosophy was dangerous to faith, and that which was dangerous to faith was dangerous to the continuation of Islamic empires (for which faith is the basis).

- Mysticism: Mysticism was the hallmark of the Sufis whose numbers and political strength were growing exponentially as they formed into *tariqas* (brotherhood). The Sufis taught that at every moment the universe was annihilated and re-created, and that God and the Universe were one (not distinct as "orthodox" Islamic theology holds.) Jalal al Rumi (1207-1273) was composing his beautiful Sufi poetry; he was a Mawlawi/Melevi dervish.

- Education: The Turks opened many madrassas (religious schools), but the *madrassas* were for study in Qur'anic law, and so did not teach the (physical) sciences and philosophy. The m*adrassas'* mission was to turn out *qadi* (judges) and *ulama* (religious scholars) for societies attempting to live by the correct understanding of the Qur'an, *hadith* (sayings of Mohammed), and *Shari'a.*

17. The 15th century saw the fall of Constantinople (1453) and the Byzantine Empire to the Ottoman Turks led by Sultan Memed II "the Conqueror" (1432-1481).

- Sultan and caliph, Suleiman "the Lawgiver" (1494-1566; Europeans called him Suleiman "the Magnificent") established an empire that stretched from the Danube to Egypt to Iraq. This empire will exist in one form or another until the end of World War I.

- The Ottomans established a millet/*dhimmi* system in which non-Muslims were allowed to rule their own communities with their own set of laws so long as those laws did not infringe on *Shari'a* or other functions of the state.

- Islam reached the numerous islands of Southeast Asia through the activities of Muslim traders and Sufi proselytizers. Sufis were viewed as healers—they practiced Aristotelian medicine—and this influenced many prospective converts.

- Columbus' discovery warranted only a brief notice in *Dar al Islam.*

18. The *Reconquista* (led by the *Reyes Catholicos,* Ferdinand and Isabella) was completed in 1492.

- The Spanish Inquisition forced Muslims and Jews to flee from Spain or convert to Catholicism.

- In 1492 throughout Spain the news was that there were western continents. Sea explorers had already brought to Portugal the news that the "Spice Islands" could be reached by sailing around the Cape of Good Hope. The Portuguese began setting up trading posts and small, fortified towns along the western coast of Africa and the coast of India after defeating Muslim navies.

Recall:

Bayt al Hikma, caliph/khalifah, Dar al Harb, dhimmi, falsafah, fiqh, fitnah, ilm, jizra, Kaaba, , madhab, madrassa, qadi, Rashidun, riddah, salafiist, Shari'a, Sufis, sultan, tariqa, umma, za'iraja

Reflect:

Look at a geographical/geological map of the Arabian Peninsula. Determine what are the various land-forms, rain patterns, and vegetation.

Respond:

1. What in Mohammed's message would have been appealing to Arab peoples?

2. Who were the Byzantines and the Sassanians? Cite their respective religions.

3. What characteristics of early Islam and the Arab peoples would have aided "the armies of Islam" " to spread so rapidly throughout North Africa and Asia?

4. Why did Islam face civil war so soon after its founding? What was the outcome of this strife?

5. What is a theocracy? Can the term be successfully applied to early *Dar al-Islam* or is it a misleading application?

6. Why might one call the 8th to the 13th centuries Islam's Golden Age?

7. What forces may have caused a tarnishing of the Golden Age of Islam?

8. What were the socio-political effects of the "fall" of Constantinople in 1453?

9. What was the situation in Spain in 1492?

10. What were the three great Muslim empires and where were they located?

LECTURE 6

A HISTORY OF ISLAM: 1600 TO 2011

1. Though Dar al Islam was slowly moving into a defensive posture against Western/Christian geographical, cultural, and economic inroads in the 15th century, three great Muslim empires controlled much of central Asia, northern India, and a good portion of the Mediterranean basin.

   - In India, Pakistan, and Afghanistan, the Mughal Empire (1526-1857) produced many great cultural achievements in the arts, architecture, fashion, and letters. It was primarily Sunni Muslim, but much religious freedom was granted to other faiths. Famously, the ruler Shah Jihan (1592-1666) built the Taj Mahal (*taj* = crown, *mahal* = love) as a mausoleum for his beloved, Mumtaz Mahal.

   - The Ottoman Empire (1299-1923) stretched from the Danube to Iraq and across the Middle East and North Africa to Algeria. It was primarily Sunni Muslim.

   - The Safavid Empire (1502-1736) in Iran and Iraq established Shi'ite Islam over a citizenry made up of Arabs, Azerbaijanis, Greeks, Georgians, Kurds, and Persians. The Battle of Chaldiran (west of Tabriz) created a boundary between the Ottoman Empire and Iran which remains today as Iran's border with Turkey.

   - Sufis and Muslim businessmen brought Islam to Southeast Asia and Indonesia.

2. In addition to the taking of Spain by the *Reyes Catolicos* Isabella and Ferdinand in the 15th century, Muslims were being forced out of southern France, Italy, and Sicily and were facing the establishment of Portuguese entrepôts along the African and Indian coasts.

   - In the late 16th and early 17th centuries, the Dutch captured Muslim and Portuguese ports. The East Indies became the Dutch East Indies.

3. The Treaty of Carlowicz (1699) spelled the end of Ottoman expansion into Europe and was seen by the Ottomans as a great defeat. Ottoman Hungary

was ceded to Austria, and this was the genesis of the Austrian-Hungarian (Christian) Empire.

- The 17th century saw Western Europe moving into the Modern Age. Hierarchical, vertical structures in politics, religion, and scientific thought were being replaced by horizontal interpretations of reality. The new "Mechanical Philosophy" was grounded in the thinking of Copernicus, Galileo, Newton, Gassendi, Luther, Francis Bacon, Descartes, Hobbes, and Locke.

4. The 18th through 19th centuries saw an accelerated European expansion into Africa, India, and the Far East (as well as into the "New World"), and entrepôts developed into fortified towns. With the Industrial Revolution of the 18th century, European factories required an ever-growing supply of raw materials, and a good many of these materials came from areas that had Muslim cultures.

- Protestant missionaries became active in many areas of *Dar al Islam*, along with traders, businessmen, and advisors.

- Weak sultans and *amirs* (military commander) easily fell to the persuasive devices of enterprising Westerners. With only a few exceptions, colonization and control of Islamic lands by the West occurs as a natural development of industrial-commercial economics—in general, it was not a matter of warfare and military suppression. The West needed raw materials for its factories and markets in which to sell finished goods. Muslim lands (and the "New World" were ripe for both raw production and retail buying.

- In 1798 Napoleon took much of Egypt, though it would soon, along with India, become part of the British Empire.

- The outcome of the Crimean War (1853-1856) was that Russia and other European powers controlled Ottoman lands in southern Russia and the Balkans.

- The struggle over control of central Asia (Iraq, Iran, Afghanistan, and northern India) was known as "The Great Game" (1803-1907), a game played out by Russia and Great Britain.

- If not outright colonization, some areas of the world became ordered as (European) "spheres of influence."

5. In the 19th century and early 20th, European diplomats particularly focused on the "sick man of Europe," the Ottoman Empire, which was tottering. The "near Orient" (also called "the Levant"), the Maghreb, Egypt, the Balkans, and southern Russia appeared to be ready for takeover by European powers.

- European artists were fascinated by the culture they found in Muslim countries that ringed the Mediterranean Sea, and so produced a great many Orientalist paintings in a romantic style. The vision that their canvases inspired in viewers made the Muslim world look decadent but erotic.

- The British upper classes romanticized the Greek areas of the Ottoman Empire and developed the idea that Greece should be separated from the Ottomans, so that the Greeks would have their own homeland.

- Also concerned about the fate of the Marionite Christians in the Lebanon, Europeans intervened there to set up a homeland for Marionites. Slightly less than half of Ottoman Lebanon would be Muslim and half would be Marionite Christian.

- European intellectuals, writers, and diplomats were concerned with the fate of the Jews in Poland and Russia, but also in Damascus where a pogrom took place in the early 1800s. This inspired the homeland concept for Jews, soon to be called Zionism.

- With the invention of the internal combustion engine in the mid-19th century, the control of oil-producing lands became the major concern of many Western nations.

6. In 1914 WWI began in the ethnically and religiously mixed Balkans. The outcome would be the end of the Ottoman Empire and the League of Nations' dividing up the Middle East and North Africa into nation-states on the European model of France, Germany, Italy, and so on.

- Each new nation-state would be overseen in its development by the French (Lebanon, Syria, Algeria), Great Britain (Palestine, Transjordan, Egypt, India), Belgium (Congo), and the Netherlands (Malaysia).

- The homeland concept for various ethnic groups was also put forward. This was supposed to insure a safe haven for specific ethnic groups through the physical separation of warring parties (alternately, others might read this plan as a "divide and conquer" strategy by the European powers.)

- Greeks and Turks were separated: Greeks in the new Republic of Turkey (founded 1923) going to Greece and Turks in Greece going back to Turkey. In 1921 the division of Ireland constituted a similar homeland/security concept.

- Arabia became Saudi Arabia with fixed boundaries. Syria and Iraq were also given fixed borders.

- The Balkans remained a firebox of hatreds among Roman Catholics, Greek Orthodox, Muslims, and Jews.

- Zionists pushed for a homeland, and Lord Balfour issued a "white paper" supposedly guaranteeing this.

7. Between WWI and WWII events worldwide stalled developing political relations between Europe and the Middle East and worsened socio-economic conditions in Muslim states.

- The newly powerful United States failed to join the League of Nations, thereby weakening the League from its very beginning.

- The Roaring Twenties, alternately the Jazz Age, turned Westerners away from world affairs.

- 1929 brought the ten-year Great Depression.

- 1930s saw the rise of the Hitler, Mussolini, and fascism as imagined ideological saviors.

- 1939 to 1945 brought WWII, a war that resulted in the deaths of 63,000,000 people and the Holocaust.

8. After WWII the United Nations again promoted the homeland concept. In 1948 the United Nations determined that Palestine would be partitioned into a Jewish state and an Arab state.. Northern India and parts of southeast Afghanistan would become Pakistan (a homeland for Muslims) and India would be kept for Hindus.

- Israel became a state through a majority vote by the United Nations.

9. Yet what all this entailed was a *Dar al Islam* defined not as an *umma* (unity, community), but as a variety of states fashioned by European (meaning also Christian) powers, following European dictates, and influenced by European legal systems, and European and then American cultures.

- At times the Islamic response was passive.

    i.   Passive: King Faruk (1920-1965), monarch of Egypt, was propped up by European and US powers.

- At times accepting and promoted.

    i.   Promoted: Syed Ahmad Khan(1817-1898) in India promoted the idea of a Muslim elite that would be involved in state administrative duties under the British. He helped to found the Muhammadan Anglo-Indian College in Aligarh in 1875 to teach Islam and the modern Western sciences.

    ii. Promoted: Cambridge-trained philosopher (mystical humanism), Muhammad Iqbal (1875-1938) is considered to be the intellectual founder of Pakistan—a homeland for Muslims beyond India. In his political writings he maintained that originally Islam was a social(ist) democracy built on the Qur'an.

- At times accepted, but with a unique twist.

    i.   Accepting in his own fashion: Mustafa Kemal (Ataturk, 1881-1938) established the Republic of Turkey as a secular state with a ninety per cent Muslim population.

    ii. Accepting in his own fashion Mohandas Gandhi (1869-1948), a Hindu, aided in the dream of founding an independent India.

- But at other times the reaction from *Dar al Islam* was hostile and violent. The reaction did not come from established, formal governments (frequently pawns of European powers), but from Sufi *tariqas*, a mahdi (messianic warrior), clandestine brotherhoods, or radical intellectuals.

i.   *Tariqa*: The Naqshbandiya *tariqa* (founded by al Naqshbandi, d.1389) in Turkey was strong enough to successfully oppose the Tanzimat (the Ottoman/Turkish government's attempt to modernize the state) in 1880. In 1925 two Naqshbandiya led Kurdish rebels in a rebellion against Ataturk's policies. They were suppressed but then transformed themselves into the Nur Sect (Followers of the Light, after Nursi 1873-1960) that wanted to make the modern Republic of Turkey an Islamic state.

ii.   *Tariqa*: Given the spread of British power in the Indian sub-continent and British support of the Hindu Mahrajahs, the Naqshbandiya became militant and fostered a *jihad* led by the Barelvi movement named for Ahmed Raza Khan Barelvi (1856–1921) against the Hindu Sikh.

iii.   *Tariqa*: In the Caucasus the Khalidiya branch of the Naqshbandiya fought Tsarist attempts to expand Russia. Presently, they are behind the war in Chechnya.

iv.   *Mahdi*: In 19th century Egypt the British found themselves facing the *mahdiya* Muhammad Ahmad at Khartoum. In 1883 the supposedly invincible British had to face up to the fact that General Chinese Gordon and his troops were slaughtered at Khartoum.

v.   Clandestine activity: The *Ikhwan al-Muslimun* (Islamic Brotherhood, or Society of the Muslim Brothers) was founded in 1928 by Hassan al Banna (1906-1949, Sunni Muslim) in Egypt to counter Western influence. Over the years it became increasingly radicalized,conducting assassinations and advocating the overthrow of various Arab governments. In Syria the Islamic Brotherhood attempted to undermine the governing Ba'ath Party.

vi.   Clandestine activity: In 1981 Anwar Sadat, Egyptian Premier was assassinated by the Egyptian Islamic Jihad.

vii.   Radical intellectual: Sayyid Qutb (1906-1966) went so far as to advocate the assassination of Muslim un-Islamic Muslim state leaders.

viii.   Radical intellectual: Another advocate of such Islamic radicalism was the Indian Muslim, Sayyid al-Maududi (1903-79). He held that Islam was the perfect life-religion, whereas Western society will forever be wracked by social and moral imperfections.

10.   At present, states with majority Muslim populations constantly wrestle with the influence of Western interventions and Western modernity, their own dictatorships, and mass poverty. Moreover, leaders of Arab states vie constantly with one another in attempts to determine who will be the leader of the Arab world.

- The Iranian Revolution of 1979 brought Ayatollah Khomeini (1900-1989) to power. This Islamic state sees itself as a theocracy with a hostile view of the West.

- Afghanistan is struggling with the Taliban, a group which rejects all non-Islamic influences.

- By name alone, the Arab Socialist Ba'ath Party (Ba'ath implies "resurrection" or "renaissance") in Syria and Iraq, shows how far it is from Islamist.

- On September 11, 2001, Muslim extremists flew two passenger planes into the World Trade Towers in New York City; a third plane was crashed into the Pentagon in Washington, D.C.

- Many Muslims, for the first time in history, find themselves minorities in non-Islamic countries. Though they face major adjustments in living in Western liberal or secular cultures, they frequently find themselves, paradoxically, freer to practice their faith in Western countries than in Islamic ones ruled by Muslim dictators.

11. The phrase "Arab Spring" has been used by observers of the Arab political scene to refer to popular uprisings (insurrections, civil wars, or revolutions) that in 2011 spread across Middle Eastern and North African countries. Arab Spring began in Tunisia in late 2010 and spread to Bahrain, Egypt, Jordan, Libya, Saudi Arabia, Syria, and Yemen. These uprisings were driven by people who for one reason or another had no say in their governments and believed themselves repressed. One observer of the events noted that the background of the protesters varied widely: some were university students and urban intellectuals; others were the countries' poor; and still others came from government-suppressed labor unions, political parties, or religiously-based organizations such as the Islamic Brotherhood. (What follows is a paraphrase of http://www.sourcewatch.org.)

- In Tunisia the Jasmine Revolution began when Mohammed Bouazizi lit himself on fire at a local municipal office. Because he did not have a peddler's permit, police had confiscated his cart and beat him. He wanted to file a complaint, but municipal office workers ignored him. Demonstrations began in Sidi Bouzid, Bouazizi's hometown, and then spread throughout Tunisia. Zine el-Abidine Ben Ali who became president of Tunisia in 1987 was forced from office and in October of 2011 Ennahda, a moderate Islamist party, emerged as the victor in the elections for a constitutional assembly. In part, Ennahda's platform asserts a commitment to a Western-style democracy and pledges equal opportunities in employment and education.

- Learning from the Jasmine Revolution, Egyptian activists organized a demonstration in Tahrir (Liberation) Square on January 25, to protest the Emergency Law, unemployment, poverty, and President Hosni Mubarak's government. Internet sites such as Facebook allowed the protesters to work more ably. Mubarak tried to crush protests with armed forces and plain-clothed thugs and when those tactics failed, state media called the protesters foreign agents. The protests unified Muslims and Christians, men and women. On February 11, 2011, Mubarak resigned and the army took control. In November Egypt held parliamentary elections and though there was much violence, elections went on, and Islamist parties claimed an astounding victory, receiving 65% of the total vote. The Islamic Brotherhood got 40% of the vote, and ultraconservative Salafiist groups got 25%.

- The Libyan revolt turned violent when the government responded harshly to peaceful protests. Within days of the initial protests, armed conflict broke out when protesters shot policemen and others loyal to Colonel Muammar Gaddafi in response to the killing of protesters. This was followed by further government retaliation that employed heavy artillery. Internet social media sites were used to organize people until the Libyan government shut them down.

- The United Nations passed a resolution allowing countries to take any "necessary measures…to protect civilians and civilian populated areas under threat of attack." This was followed by a NATO-led aerial bombardment of Gaddafi's army. As a result of clashes between pro- and anti-Gaddafi forces, many thousands of people were killed. Some of the fighting was tribal-based.

- Colonel Qaddafi was in power since 1969, but in October 2011 he was hunted down by rebel fighters in his hometown of Surt. He had been the longest-serving ruler in Africa and the Middle East.

- Dissent in Jordan began in January 2011. The protesters in Jordan did not want to oust King Abdullah; rather, the goals of the protests were lower food prices, fair elections, and an end to government corruption. King Abdullah responded by dissolving the parliament and firing Prime Minister Samir Rifai. The King met with opposition groups and expressed his readiness to address the grievances of the Jordanian people.

- The plea for democracy was first heard in Bahrain in February 2011, and it began online through social media sites. As with Cairo's Tahrir Square, Bahrain's Peal Roundabout became the symbol of the uprising. Troops from Saudi Arabia intervened to put down the insurrection. Nevertheless, several opposition parties have formed a coalition to denounce the governing regime and demand a transition to a constitutional monarchy.

- As with Jordan, demonstrations in Saudi Arabia were for more freedoms not for ousting the monarchy. The protests were relatively small and King Abdullah responded by attempting economic reforms, and surprisingly, granting women the right to vote in local elections.

- Protests in Syria faced harsh government retaliation. Protests began in January after a young man lit himself on fire and groups began organizing on social media sites. Initially the protests were small, but in March 2011, 100,000 protesters assembled in Daraa. The protesters wanted the termination of the emergency law which bans opposition political parties and called for the establishment of what the protesters viewed as basic human rights. In efforts to calm the situation, President Bashar al-Assad dissolved the government in Daraa.

As of June 2012, the onslaught by Assad has resulted in the loss of as many as fifteen thousand lives. In November the Arab League imposed sanctions on Syria as a punishment for its continuing harassment of its citizens. This action against an Arab League member state was unprecedented. As of August 2012, Syria is in a state of civil war.

- In January 2011, 16,000 Yemenites in the capital city of Sanaa protested the thirty-two year long the presidency of Ali Abdullah Saleh. Saleh had been out of the country for several months receiving medical treatment for injuries he sustained when the presidential compound had been attacked by General Ali Mohsen al-Ahmar's forces. The United Nations Security Council unanimously adopted a resolution supporting an agreement in which Saleh would receive immunity in exchange for a "transfer power to his deputy and end escalating violence." Adding fuel to the fire, Yemen is one of the poorest countries in the world.

12. The contemporary discussion has focused on bringing democracy to Islamicate states (supposedly to counter tribalism, injustice, suppression of the poor). But do Muslims want democracy and if they do, just what is a democratic state?

- In 1991 in Algeria the "first-round elections" were won by the fundamentalists and they claimed, "It's victory for Islam, not for democracy."

- So even if some Muslims want democracy, just what constitutes a democratic system?

- (See: Fact Sheet Nation-States in *Dar al Islam*.)

13. Following on Muslim tradition, at some future date the world will come to an end. There will be *madhi* who will reunite all Islamic factions and bring the faiths of the world to Islam. Then Jesus will return to kill the anti-Christ. Then will come the Last Judgment.

Recall:

amir, entrepôts, *Ikhwan al-Muslimun, mahdi,*

Reflect:

Ataturk turned Turkey West-facing. If you wanted to turn, let us say, Egypt, toward the West, what would you do? On the other hand, if you were a leader who wanted to reject Westernization, what would you do?

Respond:

1. Provide an example or two of how Europe's move into industrialization affected Muslim areas of the world?

2. What events demonstrate the chipping away of the Ottoman Empire by Napoleon and Russia?

3. What is the "homeland" concept?

4. Who promoted Western culture in *Dar al Islam*? Why?

5. Who reacted violently against Westernization of *Dar al Islam*? Why?

6. What clandestine activities were directed toward leaders of Islamicate states?

7. Why would Western states be fearful of Muslims being led by a *mahdi*?

8. What was "The Great Game"? Do you think it is still being played today? Why or why not?

9. Why is Western "pop culture" so influential across the world?

10. What does it take to have a democratic system of governing?

PHILOSOPHY, SCIENCE, AND TECHNOLOGY

1. Philosophy in its technical, academic sense, is the employment of deductive and inductive logic in a critical analysis of perplexing issues that arise in epistemology, metaphysics (first philosophy), and values.

    *   "Critical analysis" should be taken not only as the search for truth, but also as the process by which one reveals unsubstantiated assumptions, hidden biases, pseudo-science, and sophistry.

2. Science, as it is thought of today, is the experimental method, a fusion of tightly controlled experimentation, the construction of hypotheses and theories, and the application of mathematical exactitude. The fields of science include but are not limited to astronomy, physics, thermodynamics, and biology.

    *   From the late Middle Ages until the mid-19th century, the study of Nature was part of "natural philosophy," while more abstract, metaphysical speculation constituted "moral philosophy."

3. Technology is the practical application of scientific theory and discovery in such fields as agriculture, astronomy, and medicine. The invention of instruments and devices makes the application of technology possible.

    *   Technology depends on philosophers' providing a metaphysical perspective of the world, scientists who provide theories about some sub-section of that world, and inventors who work within a certain perspective of reality with a specific scientific theory.

    *   Technology provides tools to ease the work of everyday life. Ancient technology produced the wheel which produced the wagon which gave rise to the draft animal. Renaissance technology produced movable type that could be used in a printing press to produce books which aided by modern electronic theory led to the Kindle.

4. The lines between philosopher, scientist, inventor, and even theologian are not easy to draw when considering the Muslim scholars and researchers who lived during Islam's Classical Age.

- Many Muslim philosophers earned a living as doctors, map makers, and mechanical engineers.

- Some Muslim scholars held that science or rather *ilm* (knowledge, science) was limited only to what could be known for certain (actually a distinction rooted in Aristotle) and that would be Allah and the Qur'an.

5. Philosophers speculated about a broad variety of subjects including the nature of divinity, the creation of the world, human existence, and the constitution of ethical behavior. Islamic philosophers thought of *falsafah* (philosophy) in the following way:

    i.   Philosophy is the knowledge of all existing things as existents

    ii.   Philosophy is knowledge of divine and human matters

    iii. Philosophy is taking refuge in death, that is, love of death

    iv.   Philosophy is becoming God-like to the extent of human ability

    v.   Philosophy is predilection for *hikmah* (wisdom)

    - Instead of attaining agreement, they presented a variety of philosophical opinions regarding these issues, but they all claimed to being using *'aql* (intellect, reason).

    - Whatever the philosophical position taken, it always had some attachment to the Qur'an.

    - If any conclusion can be drawn from this Islamic understanding of philosophy, we can say, "Philosophy is a study which transforms the mind and the soul and which is never separated from the spiritual purity and ultimate sanctity that *hikmah* connotes in Islamic culture."

6. Caliph Ma'mun (786-833) had a dream in which Aristotle appeared and told him to study the works of the Greek philosophers. Ma'mun understood his dream to mean that he should aid in any way he could the study of Greco-Roman philosophy, *kalam* (logic; Arab scholasticism), and science. Late in life, he founded the *Bayt al Hikma* (House of Wisdom), an institution of higher learning, and there scholars lived by the principle that religious texts should accord with reason—their own and the Greeks'. (See the addendum at the end of this chapter for a summary of the Greco-Roman ideas that influenced Islamic philosophy.)

    - Ma'mun found support for his ideas in a group of rationalist theologians, the Mu'tazilites (roughly, "those who keep themselves apart"). The Mu'tazilites maintained that Allah had given people a free will and that the Qur'an was created by Allah, and as a creation, it was not quite as sacrosanct as Allah. From this it followed for the Mu'tazilites that scholars could freely subject the Qur'an to rational study and the tools of Greek logic.

    - However, the conservative Ash'arites [disciples of Abu 'l-Hasan al Ash'ari (874-936) and prominent scholars such as Ahmad ibn Hanbal

(780-855)] maintained that people were under the constant, unwavering direction of Allah and the Qur'an was Allah's eternal word, co-eternal with Allah and a part of Allah, and as such must be beyond the prying of rational analysis and interpretation.

- The Ash'arites ultimately triumphed over the Mu'tazilites. Caliphs who supported the Ash'arite position conducted a *mihnah* (inquisition) aimed at destroying the Mu'tazilites.

7. Islamic education for scholars-to-be was not a matter of going to a university and taking a series of classes and then getting a diploma. Future scholars traveled about from city to city from master to master, gaining what knowledge they could.

- Information was frequently transmitted orally, and memorization (often of entire books) was a central part of the educational process.

- Scholars were well-versed not in just one field but several, though often either the field of *fiqh* (law) or medicine was the primary one. Other fields of study included astronomy, mathematics, music, logic, and philosophy.

    Centers of learning did develop such as the *Bayt al Hikma*. Later there developed "schools" at Toledo, Cairo (the still open Al Ahzar University), and Palermo.

8. Over the centuries, *Dar al Islam* produced a great array of *faylasuf* (philosophers), scientists, inventors, social commentators, and theologians. (Only a very few of which can be cited here.)

- Much was done with Greek, Persian, Indian, and Egyptian source material by Islamic scholars heralding from these same cultural heritages during the first five or six centuries of Islam. Good work was done in astronomy, medicine, chemistry, and metaphysics during these centuries, and numerous histories of science texts and essays have reviewed and saluted this success.

- A list of the greatest the Muslim philosophers would include al-Kindi (thought of as the first Muslim philosopher, c. 805-873), al-Farabi (c. 870-950), ibn Sina (known to the West as Avicenna, 980-1037), al-Ghazzali (1058-1111), ibn Rushd (known to the West as Averroes, 1126-1198), Mulla Sadri (1571-1636), and Tariq Ramadan (1962—present).

- A list of Muslim "scientists" would include the astronomers al Khwarizmi (780-850), al Razi (865-925), and al Tusi (1201-1274); in chemistry Jabir ibn Hayyan (known as "Geber" in the West, (721-815); and in optics and the development of the scientific method, ibn al Haytham (965-1035).

- A list of social commentators would include the anthropologist al Biruni (973-1048), *mutakallimum* (roughly, "theologians") scholar ibn Taymiyyah (1263-1328), sociologist ibn Khaldun (1332-1406), and educator Sayyid Qutb (1906-1966).

- In other endeavors: inventors include al Jazari (1136-1206)—robotics; al Zahrawi (936-1034)—catgut sutures; and medical researchers, Avicenna (980-1037) and al-Rhazes (865-925).

9.   Abu Yusuf Ya'qub ibn Ishaq al-Kindi (805-873) is thought of as the first Islamic philosopher and one of the only ethnic Arab Islamic philosophers. He worked at the Abassid court in Baghdad, but when Caliph al-Mutawwakil (821-861) came to power al-Kindi fell out of favor as Mutawwakil had a strong anti-intellectualist outlook.

- Al-Kindi wrote on philosophy, logic, arithmetic, music, astronomy, geometry, cosmology, medicine, and astrology. However, his strongest writings appear to be on natural science.

- In *On First Philosophy*, he wrote: "Philosophy is the knowledge of the reality of things within people's possibility, because the philosopher's end in theoretical knowledge is to gain truth and in practical knowledge to behave in accordance with truth." He was saying that his subject matter was "the First Truth," which for him meant the first cause of everything including all other truths. He advocated the supremacy of reason and the use of the knowledge found in other cultures, especially Greek philosophy.

- In *On the Definitions of Things and Their Descriptions*, a book with a strong Aristotelian slant (for example in defining concepts as a way to explain them and in accepting Aristotle's four causes), al-Kindi philosophically defined such concepts as "finitude," "creation," and "first cause."

- As for divinity, he claimed that Allah is this First Truth, but unlike Aristotle's notion of the eternity of the World, al-Kindi maintained that Allah [who is eternal, immutable, absolutely unitary (thus having no attributes or characteristics—very neo-Platonic), and the cause of everything] created the World *ex nihilo* (Latin: "out of nothing"). Moreover, Allah is prior in time, and hence is the cause of time.

- In regard to the human being, al-Kindi held that the soul and the body were distinct, and that the soul and its cultivation were much more important than the body. The intellect (a part of the soul) survives bodily death.

- As for human behavior, al-Kindi's *On the Art of Adverting Sorrows* was greatly influenced by Epictetus's Stoic ethics. The core idea was that one should strive for freedom from worldly cares and to realize that we can be self-directed agents who through our independence are the one's responsible for our own happiness.

10.   Abu Nasr Mohammad Ibn Mohammad ibn Tarkham ibn Awzabagh al-Farabi (c. 870-950) is known as the "Father of Islamic Neo-Platonism" and "Second Master" (the first being Aristotle). He was a scholar in math, medicine, music, sociology, and philosophy. He had many followers (the "Farabian school of thought," prominent from 870 to 1023). He blended Plato, Aristotle, and

Neo-Platonism, even attempting to show that Plato and Aristotle were not often at philosophic odds (which they were).

- As for divinity, he claimed that in the case of Allah and only Allah, essence and existence are not separate. Allah completely transcends the world and so He can only be "understood" negatively ("infinite," "beyond time," etc.). Allah is Divine Reason and the source of all knowledge and wisdom in the world.

- In regard to the structure of the world and the status of human beings, al-Farabi, adopting Neo-Platonism, held that Allah emanated the world, and a hierarchy of being was the product of this emanation: Allah is "the First" and the First creates the First Intellect (the Second Being) that in its comprehension of "the First" emanates the Second Intellect (the Third Being), and this in its comprehension emanates *al-sama' al-ula* (body and soul) which is the First Heaven, and then come the fixed stars and then the tenth intelligence (the Agent Intellect) which activates human thought and produces the physical world.

- As for human behavior, Al-Farabi was deeply influenced by Plato's *Republic*, but he combined the ideas in the *Republic* with Aristotle's thesis that the good life was the happy life. The virtuous society is one in which people cooperate to gain happiness. Eternal salvation will be Allah's reward to people for achieving social happiness.

11. Abu Ali al Hasan ibn Al Haytham (965-1030), as did so many other Classical Age Muslim scholars, worked in many areas of science, but of most importance was his development of the scientific method of research.

- Al Haytham understood the value of controls when proceeding with experimentation—that an experiment must be clearly defined to know what was and was not influencing possible results.

- In his work on optics, he relied on both physics and mathematics as tools in his testing of his hypotheses.

- He understood the value of what has become known as Occam's Razor—do not unnecessarily multiply causes for a phenomenon under study.

12. Abn Ali Al Hosain Ibn Abdallah Ibn Sina (to the Latin West, "Avicenna," 980-1037) was known in medieval *Dar al Islam* as a great physician, but he was also an important philosopher who mingled Platonism, Aristotelianism, Neo-Platonism, Galenism, Farabianism, with other Greek and Islamic ideas, quite freely.

- In regard to the structure of the world and the status of human beings, ibn Sina closely follows Aristotle.

  i. The agent intellect holds matter and form together and so is the cause of natural bodies.

  ii. The celestial (sidereal) realm moves with a circular motion and the heavenly bodies are eternal and are at peaceful equilibrium.

iii.   Sub-lunar bodies are subject to generation and corruption, and the most basic bodies are the four elements. When the elements come together the objects they make up vary in proportionality of elements, and because of this, a division occurs between mineral, vegetative, animal, and humans. Moreover, the more celestial a body the more equilibrium it has, and the highest (having the most equilibrium) is the human soul which is the form of the body. The human rational soul, which is both immaterial and immutable, is divisible into the theoretical and practical.

- As for human behavior, Ibn Sina's development of practical philosophy is not only dependent on prior philosophical trends, but also on the Qur'an and *Shari'a*. He wanted to explain how people function socially.

  i.   The correct management of a city is of utmost importance.

  ii.   The proper relations within the home make for a pleasant life.

  iii. Virtuous personal behavior and the cultivation of one's soul is necessary for personal fulfillment.

- As for divinity, Allah is the necessary existent being, first cause, free from matter (hence, he is completely good as matter is the principle of evil), pure intellect and pure beauty. Everything emanates from Allah eternally, hence an eternal universe--no *creatio ex nihilo*.

13.   Abu Hamid Muhammad Ibn Muhammad Al-Ghazzali (1058-1111) was a student of Iman al-Juwayni from whom he learned the Ash'arite outlook. A jurist, theologian, and mystic, he fought against what he viewed as the errors of the philosophers, though because of the depth of his thinking, he really was a philosopher himself. His major philosophical work is *Tahafut al-Falasifah* (*The Incoherence of the Philosophers*). It is al-Ghazzali's insights that came to constitute the "orthodox" (if there is one) position in Islam, and he has been given the title "The Proof of Islam."

- In his attack on philosophers, al-Ghazzali argued that philosophers cannot prove the truths of (a) God's creation of the world, and (b) the soul's spiritual substance. He claimed, moreover, that the writings of philosophers show they are infidels because of what they assert.

  i.   The world is eternal (from Aristotle).

  ii.   Allah does not know particular things and events (from Plato).

  iii. That there is no bodily resurrection and individual souls as individuals are not immortal (both Plato and Aristotle).

- Knowledge is dependent on divine *ilhan* (illumination) and divine inspiration, and it persuades both the mind and heart, and this the philosophy of the "philosophers" (really Aristotle's syllogistic logic) cannot do. We can doubt our senses for they deal with appearances, but we cannot doubt revelation (the Qur'an).

- As for divinity, Al-Ghazzali maintained *tawhid* (unity—the absolute unity of God), the eternity of the Qur'an, and that the anthropomorphic descriptions of God in the Qur'an are accurate. Allah wills all things and so fire burns cotton, but only if Allah wills it. In other words, there are no necessary causal relations.

- As for human behavior, Al-Ghazzali's life was a model of asceticism (rejection of worldly goods), repentance, and fear of Allah (a silent satisfaction with and an acceptance of God's decrees). He held that caliphs as supreme religious leaders and sultans as supreme political leaders must work together to bring peace to a Muslim empire. Revolts of any kind were wrong and not to be tolerated, and this meant the maintenance of peace at all costs.

14. Abu Muhammad Jabir ibn Aflah (1100-1150), known to the Latin West as "Geber," was an astronomer and mathematician. His book *Correction of the Almagest* had a great impact on astronomers of all three Abrahamic faiths. His work was a criticism and correction of the Roman astronomer Ptolemy (90-168) whose *Mathematical Treatise* had been the standard work in astronomy for a thousand years.

    - An excellent mathematician he developed trigonometry to better plot the movements of the planets.

    - He adjusted Ptolemy's placement of the planets to a more mathematical exact spacing in the universe.

15. Abu'l-Walid Muhammad Ibn Ahmad Ibn Rushd [known in the West as Averroes and called "the Commentator" (on Aristotle), 1126-1198] was more of a jurist and physician than a philosopher, and in the sciences he worked in astronomy, cosmology, and medicine (he maintained that key to health are good digestion, good bowel movement, and avoidance of fruits and herbs). His *Tahafut al-Tahafut* (*Incoherence of the Incoherence*) attempted to refute the *mutakallimun* led by al-Ghazzali. His philosophical writings are a synthesis of Almohad Islam and Aristotle.

    - Ibn Rushd's philosophical position could be summarized in six surprisingly un-Islamic propositions.

        i. We can say nothing about Allah's essence for it is beyond human ability to know, but we can know much about Allah through His actions.

        ii. The world is eternal.

        iii. Allah does not know of particular objects or events.

        iv. There is no providence, and so humans have free will.

        v. Because the active intellect of each person and the world are one, there is no individual moral responsibility.

        vi. Given that the active intellect is one there is no individual immortality.

- Though ibn Rushd believed that philosophy and theology could be harmonized, he was interpreted as propounding a doctrine of "double truth," namely, that if philosophy and theology contradicted each other on some point, both understandings though opposites could be true at the same time.

16. Al Jazari (1136-1206) inventor, artist, astronomer, and mathematician, wrote *Book of Knowledge of Ingenious Mechanical Devices*.

   - A major invention that could be employed in a variety of ways was the camshaft—a wood or metal shaft onto which were affixed cams (off-center wheels) for activating motion in a given procession.

   - He designed clocks, a mechanical music box, and a double-action suction pump.

17. Taqi al Din Ahmad ibn Taymiyyah (1263-1328) was a prominent *mutakallimum* who lived through the devastation of the Mongol invasions. His response was a call to his fellow Muslims to return to a "true Islamic life," and second, to commit themselves to *jihad* of the sword.

   - Theologically, he saw the Mongols as the instrument of Allah's punishment of the Muslim *umma* which had turned away from a true Islamic life.

   - Practically, a "true Islamic life" dictated that all the *adat/urf* that had crept into the Islamic faith over the centuries had to be jettisoned. The first years of the faith, when the faith was at its purest, had to be returned to. The call to return to the beginnings of the faith is called *salaf* or *salafiism.*

   - Second, the "true Islamic life" required a strong emphasis on *jihad* of the sword. *Jihad* could be carried on even against other Muslims, if those Muslims instituted laws and rulings that did not follow *Shari'a.*

   - Ibn Taymiyyah's writings were the inspiration to Muhammad ibn Abdel Wahab, the 18th century founder of ultra-conservative Wahabism, and at present to a variety of Muslim movements such as the Muslim Brotherhood and Al Qaeda.

18. Abu Zayd 'Abd al-Rahman ibn Khaldun al-Hadrami (1332-1406) was born in Tunis and during his life traveled widely in the Mahgreb and the Middle East. He was a member of the Sultan of Morocco's *ulama;* a diplomat; and the author of *Muqaddimah* (*Prolegomena*), an important sociological study of Muslim medieval life. He experienced firsthand the effects on Muslim populations of the Black Death (1348-49).

   - Ibn Khaldun wanted the *Muqaddimah* to be a history of human civilization and social organization that would explain the conditions that affect civilizations. He concluded that *'asabiyyah* (social group feeling) is the driving force in society, a force which could culminate in taking over the state.

   - Ibn Khaldun theorized that the tribal state is composed of a central core of the ruling elite. Circling this core are tribes/clans/families that are closely associated with the elites and pay no taxes, but act as tax collectors and enforcers. The next farther out circle is composed of tribes/clans/families that are taxed but are under the protection of the state. Finally, furthest out are tribes/clans/families that have not been subdued, pay no taxes, and live in an uncivilized/non-civic setting absorbed in antagonism, local feuds, and constant acts of revenge toward each other. Nevertheless, if these outmost tribes ("the "wolves") ever coalesce, *'asabayyah*, under a central leadership and unifying religion/dogma/ideology, they will overturn the ruling elites and become the new tribal state leaders.

- Ibn Khaldun attacked formal logic (Aristotelian logic) and Neo-Platonism. He criticized logic on the grounds that rationality could only get one so far, and reason/logic as employed by philosophers was constantly being pushed beyond its limits.

- Ibn Khaldun is clearly in the camp of the Ash'arites and al Ghazzali. Philosophy is dangerous to faith, and that which is dangerous to faith is dangerous to the continuation of Islamic empires (of which faith is the basis).

19. The mystical side of Islamic faith and worship is found in the Sufi tradition. The Sufis represent *tasawwuf* (Islamic mysticism), and they are found throughout the various Muslim sects, whether Shi'ite, Sunni, Ismaili, Alawite, or others. They are mystics who believe they are closer to Allah than other Muslims, because they strive (some claim to accomplish) for a direct *gnosis* or even communion with Allah. Some Sufis claim to find God within and then become one with Allah—claims that other Muslims have at times called heretical. Al-Muhasibi (781-857), a Baghdad mystic, wrote of his quest for "nearness to the Beloved." Al-Muhasibi is only the first of a long line of Sufi poets.

- The origins of the Sufis can be traced to ascetic disciplines developed in response to growing wealth and worldliness of the early, expanding Muslim empire, yet this movement did not begin to get systematized and organized until the 9th century.

- Many Sufis shun money and material things.

- Ibn Arabi (1165-1240), the classical Sufi author who wrote *The Meccan Revelations*, *The Essentials of Wisdom*, and *The Interpreter of Dreams*, combined Muslim and Neo-Platonist thought, de-rationalized the two and produced a mystical philosophy. Basing his philosophy on intuitive revelation, he said that the human mind was an (down-graded) emanation of Allah's mind, emphasizing again the oneness of the universe.

- The most famous poet-philosopher Sufi is Jalal al Rumi (1207-1273). Rumi proclaimed the oneness of universe in wild love poetry.

- Sufis belong to *tariqa* (orders, brotherhoods) such as the Mawlawi, Tijaniyya, Sanusiyya, and the Naqshbandiya.

- Some Sufi *pirs* claim magical powers—frequently powers of healing illnesses. After their death they might be looked on as saints with miraculous powers while their tombs are thought to have *baraka* (especial power). Some study and practice Aristotelian medicine or holistic medicine based on diet and herbs.

20. Muhammad Ibn Ibrahim Al-Qawami al-Shirazi (1572-1640), commonly known as Mulla Sadra, and given the honorific title Sadr al-Din Shirazi (Pundit of Religion), was a mystic and theosophist. Mulla Sadra claimed to have had a direct experience (the opening of "the eye of the heart") of Ultimate Reality.

- In regard to epistemology, Mulla Sadra said that there were three paths to enlightenment: revelation, demonstration or intellection, and mystical vision.

- In regard to the structure of the world, it is best understood by citing as an analogy the sun and its rays. The rays of sunlight appear to be distinct from the sun itself though really this is not the case, because everything is united and One. And yet as the rays are less than the sun, the things of the World exist in a hierarchical schema. There is a Great Chain of Being, which, nevertheless, is unified.

- Everything is to be understood as acts of existence and not objects that exist. While the Sufis taught that at every moment the universe is annihilated and re-created, Mulla Sadra claimed a doctrine of trans-substantial motion in which everything is in constant motion or becoming, meaning that an object keeps acquiring new forms added to a substantive (matter) base until it finally reaches formal maturity (its archetypal, final, finished, predestined goal). Each state of development contains all its former forms (rather than losing them or sloughing them off.)

- The doctrine of trans-substantial motion also applies to human beings. We develop from fertilized egg, gaining form after form, until there is reached a conjoining with Ultimate Reality which is God in the World of the Archetypes. As for divinity, Allah knows all things; nothing, not even an atom, is hidden.

- There will be bodily resurrection after death, though the bodies will be especially subtle and "woven" of the actions that the individual person performed in this world. Evil souls will choose Hell because of the evil actions of which their afterlife bodies are woven.

21. Muslim achievements and insights began to slide into a serious decline beginning in the 13th century. Causes can be found in the areas of faith, warfare, and education, and a misunderstanding of what constitutes science and philosophy. By the 18th century, Dar al Islam had fallen far behind the West in most areas of economic and scientific development.

- Dar al Islam never went through the socio-political revolutions caused by the Renaissance, Protestant Reformation, Enlightenment, or Industrial Revolution as did the West.

- The first known effort to translate Western scientific writings and bring them to Indians (either Muslim or Hindu) was conducted by Sir Sayyid Ahmad Khan (1817-1898), founder of the Scientific Society at Ghazipur, and this was in the mid-19th century.

22. The Egyptian Sayyid Qutb (1906-1966) spent the early part of his career as an educator, but became radicalized during a sojourn in the United States (1948 -1950), and upon his return to Egypt, became a member of the Muslim Brotherhood.

- In 1949 he wrote *Social Justice in Islam* the thesis of which was *tawhid*, a theme found earlier in the writings of al Ghazzali. He held that the universe and Nature proceed from Allah's will, and that Nature and humankind are united in harmony, and therefore no antagonism can or should exist between man and his surroundings.

- He did not believe that his native Egypt was being ruled in Islamic fashion, but knowing that Islam expressly forbids assassinating an Islamic ruler, he developed the principle that if the ruler of an Islamic nation doesn't implement Islamic laws, the ruler is not a Muslim but an infidel, and infidels may be killed (according to Islamic laws) with impunity. (This position appears to be an extension of the ideas of ibn Taymiyyah.) His writings have been a boon to radical Islamists, and have been widely circulated among al Qaeda.

23. The contemporary European Islamic scholar Tariq Ramadan (1962-present) was named by *Time Magazine* as one of the hundred most important innovators of the 21st century. He taught at the College of Geneva and as professor of Islamic studies at Fribourg, Switzerland. Hassan al Banna, founder of the Islamic Brotherhood, was his maternal grandfather.

- Ramadan proposes a modernizing of Islam, but not an accommodation to or acceptance of all things Western. He proposes that Islam have vast and global overarching principles for dealing with consumer capitalism and world poverty. The idea is to develop a Western Muslim as opposed to an Arab Muslim, African Muslim, or Indonesian Muslim.

- He holds that the notion that the West is *dar al harb* must be abandoned and be supplanted as *dar al shahada*, the land where a Muslim announces his/her faith and testifies to his/her faith. Muslims must fully enter the social and political spheres of whatever country they live in. They must not act as a ghetto-ized minority.

24. Fouad Ajami (1945-present) is a Lebanese-American and the Director of the Middle East Studies Program at Johns Hopkins University. He has written several books, one of the more important being *The Dream Palace of the Arabs: A Generation's Odyssey*.

- He was the most influential Arab-American scholar in terms of the President George W. Bush's administration and was a supporter of the war in Iraq.

- He is viewed by many Muslim intellectuals as a "conservative" thinker.

- He rejects Huntington's thesis of a "class of civilizations" as focused too narrowly on culture, thereby not taking account of national politics and that modernism and secularism are here to stay.

Recall:

al-sama' al-ula, 'aql, Ash'arite, 'asabiyyah, caliph, Dar al Islam, Dar al Harb, creatio ex nihilo, faylasuf, hikmah, ilhan, ijtihad, kalam, mashiyyat Allah, mihnah, mutakallimum, Mu'tazalites, *polis, qadi, taqlid, tasawwuf, tawhid, za'iraja*

Reflect:

In a short essay compare and contrast a few ideas of Ajami and Ramadan on the future of Islam.

Respond:

1. In what ways did Greek philosophy influence Islamic philosophy?

2. In what ways did Islamic religion influence Islamic philosophy?

3. Other than al-Ghazzali and thinkers after ibn Rushd (Averroes), compare and contrast the various philosophical positions of the Islamic philosophers.

4. In what ways was Averroes a radical thinker?

5. How did al-Ghazzali and ibn Khaldun put a "damper" on rationalist philosophical thinking?

6. Why did science and philosophy come to an end in *Dar al Islam*?

7. What can be said about the mysticism of the Sufis, Ibn Khaldun, Mulla Sadra?

8. Sayyid Qutb obviously did not like what he saw in America. How near or off the mark was he in his assessments of American culture?

9. In a couple of sentences explain Huntington's phrase "a clash of civilizations."

10. Cite an area of science that benefited from Muslim research.

ADDENDUM

The great age of Islamic philosophy is 833 to 1200, and a significant portion of Islamic philosophy is rooted in the ideas of two Greek philosophers, Plato and Aristotle, and a Greco-Roman, Plotinus. Given this fact, a sampling of those ideas that had an impact on Muslim philosophers would be useful for a student of Islamic philosophy to review.

PLATO (Athens, Greek, 427 to 347 B.C.E.)

1. Plato said that there were two worlds, a World of Appearance and a World of Forms, and the latter was the more real.

    *   The World of Appearance is daily experiences; it is what is sensed. Always changing, its contents are forever in the process of becoming something else. The World of Appearance is less than real, there is no truth or factuality to be found there, but it is not imaginary. The World of Appearance contains multiples of particular things.

    *   The World of Forms is fully real; it is what truly exists and is completely independent of any human thoughts about it. A form is immutable, universal, eternal, and true. All particular triangles, for example, in the World of Appearances are triangles only as they are related in some fashion to the form of a triangle.

    *   The forms are known by the exercise of the highest powers of the human mind. The highest form is the form of the Good.

2. Plato claimed that soul and body are distinct: when the body dies the soul goes on to the World of the Forms for a period of time and then is re-installed in another body. A famous analogy explaining the relationship between soul and body is that the soul is to the body as a captain is to a ship.

    *   Humans have a rational, spirited, and appetitive soul. An animal has a spirited and appetitive soul, while plants had only a appetitive soul.

3. In the *Republic*, Plato gives his vision of a good city-state.

    *   Plato's asserts that the ideal society is composed of three social classes, each with their own unique function, purpose, and virtue. These classes are the Guardians (philosopher-kings), Auxiliaries (soldiers), and Workers.

4. Plato has little to say about Nature and physical phenomena, because these are a part of the World of Appearance of which it is impossible to say anything true. However, in the *Timeaus*, a dialogue Plato wrote toward the end of his life, he presents his conception of how the world and its contents were created.

    *   The universe comes into existence when the Demiurge (a less than supreme maker-god) cuts two bands out of the sphere of the Receptacle and fashions these into an "X" pattern. Evil is the function

of that which gets in the way of the Demiurge's work, namely, the raw material of the Receptacle. In this scheme, form (finer, spiritual stuff) is good, while material (bodily stuff) is less than good, though not necessarily evil.

ARISTOTLE (Athens, Greek, 384 to 322 B.C.E.)

1. Aristotle has been called the first scientist because of his interest in biology, physics, and astronomy. As Plato's thinking was "other-world" oriented (the World of Forms), Aristotle was oriented to "this world". With broad interests, he wrote on metaphysics, physics, biology, astronomy, ethics, physiology, psychology, politics, and rhetoric, and produced the first formal system of logic.

    *   Aristotle's developed a fool-proof tool for reasoning—syllogistic logic. Even if its application was limited, in many cases it allowed one to reason validly from premises to a conclusion.

2. Though Aristotle agreed with Plato regarding the existence of forms, he placed the form in objects. He rejects Plato's suggestion of an actual World of Forms.

    *   Objects are composed of matter and form, and are describable by citing four explanatory causes: material, efficient, formal, and final.

    *   Objects that are alive fall into one of three categories: human, animal, or vegetation. Humans have a rational, sensitive, and vegetative soul. An animal has a sensitive and vegetative soul, while plants have only a vegetative soul.

3. Aristotle provided an extensive explanation of change and motion.

    *   In change, things move from potentiality to actuality. Over time objects are driven by a form-in-potentiality to completely actualize that form.

    *   The primary provider of motion to the entire cosmos is the Unmoved Mover, who is perfection and complete in itself.

    *   The law of all motion is "A thing remains at rest unless acted upon."

4. Aristotle's astronomy is geocentric, and the universe is a composition of a sub-lunar realm and a sidereal real.

    *   In the sub-lunar realm earth, air, fire, and water (the four Greek elements) are mixed together, and therefore impure and imperfect.

    *   The moon and beyond exist in the sidereal realm which is perfect and whose substance is a fifth element, aether—a pure and perfect substance. Here the planets, the stars, the moon and the sun move in perfect circle. At the outermost reaches of the heavens is the Unmoved Mover.

PLOTINUS (Alexandria, Rome, Greco-Roman, 204 to 270 C.E.)

1. Frequently considered the last great Classical philosopher, Plotinus developed a mystical philosophy, Neo-Platonism.

2. Plotinus claimed that the One is the source of all existence.

   • The One is God and all thing flow out of this divine being; this is the Doctrine of Emanation.

   • The One creates of necessity, since it simply overflows with goodness and existence.

   • Though God is One, the One also contains Mind and Soul. This is a trinitarian god.

3. Since the One is completely good and the source of all that exists, existence is good.

   • Evil is a lack of the One's existence, and therefore evil is a lack of goodness and being. Evil is non-existence, or rather a privation of God. Some philosopher's say that this lack is to be identified with material (bodily) substance.

4. Plotinus believed that human beings are free to either turn toward the One (more goodness and existence) or turn away from the One (toward evil).

   • A more materialistic person cares for bodily things and hence is turning away from the One, or in other words, soul/spiritual is good, body/sensuality is evil.

   • A more spiritual person works to purify his or her soul and this is turning toward the One

   • Those who turn toward the One might achieve a mystical union with the divinity—this is human salvation.

A SAMPLING OF ISLAMIC PHILOSOPHICAL ISSUES INFLUENCED BY GRECO-ROMAN PHILOSOPHY

1. Issue: The creation of the world. Responses: (a) no creation as both Allah and the World are eternal; (b) Allah created the World out of nothing (*creatio ex nihilo*); (c) Allah emanated the World out of Himself; (d) beyond human knowledge.

2. Issue: Knowledge of Allah. Responses: (a) Physical descriptions of Allah are accurate, but are not comprehensible; (b) physical descriptions are to be understood metaphorically; (c) Allah is beyond human comprehension except where clearly revealed in the Qur'an.

3. Issue: Allah's relation to World. Responses: (a) Allah knows every particular event and action; (b) Allah knows universal properties and essences.

4. Issue: The status of the Qur'an. Responses: (a) the Qur'an is a creation in time; (b) the Qu'an is the Word of Allah and is eternal and uncreated.

5. Issue: Free will and determinism. Responses: (a) people have free will; (b) there is free will, but it is limited; (c) all things are completely in Allah's hands and completely pre-determined

6. Issue: The physical structure of the universe. Responses: (a) variations on Aristotle and Ptolemy's astronomy and physics.

7. Issue: The structure of society and city. Responses: (a) variations on either Plato's or Aristotle's descriptions of the microcosm and macrocosm.

LECTURE 8

LAW AND JURISPRUDENCE

1. Islamic nations to one degree or another follow a legal and moral code referred to as *Shari'a*. *Shari'a* is considered to be a normative ideal and a way of life; it is Allah's directives for a perfect set of laws for living one's life in a sacred fashion. Yet, there seems to be at least two different understandings of what constitutes *Shari'a*.

    *   By 900 *Shari'a* had developed as a comprehensive set of rules and sanctions covering almost every aspect of human life. Both the public and private spheres from personal hygiene to social relations to political practices were rule-governed activities.

    *   One understanding is that *Shari'a* is Allah's eternal and universal laws for regulating the behavior of all things, but especially the personal, social, and religious behaviors of human beings. From such universal principles, *fiqh* (Islamic substantive law, e.g., particular, practical laws people follow in their daily lives) and jurisprudence (how legal matters are conducted in court) are derived through various ways by the *ulama*.

    *   A second understanding of *Shari'a* claims that it is the actual body of *fiqh* and jurisprudence.

    *   *Shari'a* covers *ibadat* (relations between people and God), and *muamala* (peoples' relations to other people).

    *   Some Muslim states have both a Western court system and a *Shari'a* court system exercising *Shari'a* law.

2. Possibly, a good way of understanding the difference between *sharia* legal theory and the Western legal theory is to see *Shari'a* as rooted in tribal culture and Western theory as state-based.

    *   In *Shari'a*, the litigants in a criminal case or civil suit face off against each other in the courtroom, while in Western jurisprudence, the defendant in a criminal case faces off against the state.

    *   In *Shari'a*, in the case of a killing or murder, if the family of the deceased accepts a payment of some sort, the case is considered

settled. In other cases "an eye for an eye" is literally applied. In Western law, the accused, if found guilty, faces state-determined sanctions. In civil cases (law suits), in the Western system, settlements are determined by the court, or between litigants "before the case goes to court."

3. The constitution of *fiqh* and jurisprudence has developed over time and continues to develop to meet new situations. Moreover, the body of laws and procedures depends on several sources for its development. The sources of *fiqh* and jurisprudence include the following:

    * Qur'an: The literal Word of God, the Qur'an contains revelations of a religious, ethical, and political nature from both Mohammed's Meccan and Medinan periods.

    * *Hadith*: The *hadith* are divinely inspired words of Mohammed, but are not in the Qur'an.

    * *Sunna:* The *sunna* are the stories about Mohammed's practices and teachings.

4. Within a hundred years of Mohammed's death, there were so many *hadith* and *sunna* being cited that Mohammed would have had to have lived a dozen lifetimes in order to have said and done them all. In the 9th century Muslim scholars developed a science of *hadith*, a way of substantiating the validity and use of a *hadith* and *sunna*.

    * Some *hadith* are considered *sahih* (safe, reliable, authentic), while some *hadith* are considered *hasan* (okay), and others are *diaif* (unreliable). However, there are many gradations of reliability between the two extremes.

    * The *ulama* determine the reliability of *hadith* by ascertaining:
        i.   internal consistency
        ii.   the chain of *isnad* (chain of transmission)
        iii. the number of scholarly testifiers from different legal traditions as to its being an actual *hadith*

    * There are several different sets of *hadith* found in several distinct collections.

5. Different *ulamas* have differing opinions as to how the Qur'an and *hadith* are to be read, interpreted, and applied.

    * *qiyas*: Analogical reasoning from an established norm.

    * *ijma*: The consensus of the learned people of the religious community.

    * *taqlid*: Very closely following fiqh and jurisprudence of a well-established *madhab* (school of law and jurisprudence)

    * *ijtihad*: A looser or new interpretation of the Qur'an or *hadith*. (If an interpretation is too radical, it may be seen as bid'at (a reprehensible innovation unwarranted by the Qur'an or *hadith*).

- *adat* or *urf*: These are local time-tested customs which may occasionally influence the content of substantive law.

- *maslaha*: "The Common Good"--laws made for the good of the community when there is little guidance from Qur'an or *hadith*.

6. There are four major *madhab*s in Islam. Different Islamic states follow different schools of jurisprudence. These *madhab*s include the following:

- Hanafi School, founded by Abu Hanifa (699-767), is viewed as the most liberal of the four *madhab*s. In the Sunni tradition, its scholarship puts more emphasis on reason than the other schools. It is prominent throughout *Dar al Islam*, but especially so in Turkey and India.

- Maliki School, named for Malik ibn Anas (714-796), exists within Sunni Islam, and its teachings are followed in Africa, Saudi Arabia, United Arab Emirates, and Kuwait. It bases its legal pronouncements on the Qur'an, *hadith*, and the rulings of the *Rashidun*.

- Shafi'ite School, founded by Muhammad Idris ibn al-Shafii (767-820), bases its Sunni legal pronouncements on the Qur'an, the *sunna* and *hadith*, *ijma*, and *qiyas*. The Shafi'ite *madhab* is prominent in Indonesia and many other places, and approximately thirty per cent of Muslims ascribe to it.

- Hanbali School, founded by Ahmad ibn Hanbal (780- 855), is the smallest of the four *madhab*s, but because its home is in Saudi Arabia its influence is enormous across *Dar al Islam*.

7. The *Shari'a* courtroom and trial proceedings function in a less structured fashion than Western legal proceedings.

- The *qadi*'s job (the presiding judge) is to determine the facts of the case and what law(s) to apply. The *qadi* is an agent of the state, and his decision is binding and can be enforced by police action. He must be of high moral character.

- There are the litigants proper, the plaintiff(s) and defendant(s), but no attorneys.

- Various witnesses to the proposed action may be brought into the court room.

- Supporting documents such as the marriage contract in the case of a divorce proceeding may be presented to the *qadi*.

- There is no jury.

- The *qadi* may or may not consult with a *mufti* (legal scholar). The *mufti*'s job is to determine the law in light of competing interpretations of scripture. The *mufti* must not only be knowledgeable, he must also be of high moral character. He is concerned with specific applications of the law in specific instances.

- The *mujtahid* like the *mufti* is a scholar of the law, but he deals with less specific, more general discoveries and research of law.

8. A particular legal case could result in a *hukh* (judgment, binding decision), while a specific issue, a question of importance, could be answered by a *fatwa*.

    • A *fatwa* can be issued by any respected religious leader. [There is no formal hierarchy in the religious leadership of Islam though in some forms of Islam the *imam* (leader of a religious community) or *ayatollah* (literally "faith," but by extension "religious leader") has special status.]

    • Millions of *fatawa* ("*fatwa*" in plural form) have been issued over the years. In one century alone in northern India, the Deobondi *muftis* issued 269,215 *fatwas*. The most famous *fatwa* in recent years is the one calling for the death of Salman Rushdie (1947-present), the author of *The Satanic Verses*.

9. Some judgments issued by the Wahabis (conservative religious figures in Saudi Arabia) or the Taliban (conservative religious leaders in Afganistan) carried sanctions of *huddad* (severe punishments) such as cutting off the right hand of a thief or stoning an adulterous female.

    • Islamic morality contends that one must "command good and forbid evil." This is much stronger than the Thomistic principle that one should do good and avoid evil.

10. Among other things Islamic law forbids: *riba* (earning interest on money); intoxication and gambling; and polytheism and secularism.

    • In regard to *riba*, many serious problems arise because many large economic transactions depend on borrowing money at interest. Some Islamic scholars say that you can borrow if you are in distress and have no other option, but borrowing to buy a house does not seem to be a "distress issue." Other Islamic scholars say that you can borrow because you are in *Dar al Harb*, but borrowing to buy a house does not seem to be a "war issue." The sub-issue is whether *riba* and usury are the same.

    • Intoxication by alcohol (sometimes caffeine is included) and gambling are sins and outlawed by *Shari'a* law.

    • Secularism (when that means atheism or an agnostic life style) or polytheism is the only sin that Allah does not forgive. The sin of *shirk* [praying to other gods in addition to Allah, conjoining anything to Allah (Jesus? Holy Spirit?), or denying Allah's existence] has for its sanction, death.

    • And some things may be frowned upon, but not outlawed.

11. Of recent great interest is the treatment of women in Muslim countries. Some concerns deal with women proper; other concerns fall under the category of "family law".

    • In regard to the treatment of women, many Islamic religious scholars note the equality with which Muslim women are treated. Equality is understood as each gender has a specific and well-defined role, and though those roles are different and must be strictly adhered to, they are equal as regards commitment to the *umma*. Some Western scholars have similar opinions; others strongly disagree. The *burka* (full covering for a woman) has become a focal-point issue.

- Among other things *Shari'a* family law deals with how a *nikah* (marriage contract, or by popular implication, simply, marriage) is to be contracted, dowry, divorce, widowhood, and inheritance. The Qur'an contains many passages dealing with these issues. For example: Marriage: 24:32; Divorce: 2:226, 2:228, 2:229, 2:230, 2231; 2:240; 2:241; Widowhood: 2:233, 2:234.

12. A new question in Islamic legal theory (political philosophy) is whether Muslims can participate in or adopt as a national constitution, contemporary Western-style democracy. According to Tariq Ramadan, traditionalists and Islamic Qur'an literalists answer "no" for five reasons:

- The word "election" (as in political elections) is not a Qur'anic term. The relation between leader and individual is one of allegiance.

- In Islam one must not seek or desire to hold political office.

- A Muslim can give allegiance only to another Muslim.

- A Muslim must obey the leader, even if the leadership is far from ideal.

- The word "democracy" is not a Qur'anic term, and democracy does not respect the Islamic concept of *shura* (consultation with followers as advising, but not determining vote). In some Muslim states, the *wazir* (adviser) was an important member of the *shura*.

13. So, for modernizers (reformers), the problem is twofold: First, how to undermine traditionalist objections; and second, how to match Islamic principles with democratic ideas, principles, and forms of government.

- According to the modernizers, whatever the tack taken, it must not be withdrawal from political participation or from political associations—the rejection of victim or minority mentality.

- The distinction between *ibadat* (the relations between people and God) and *muamala* (people's relations to other people) must be recalled. Islamic *ibadat* practices maybe once and for all, but principles and laws dealing with *muamala* should be contextualized and historicized.

- *The consideration of maslaha* ("The Common Good"—laws made for the good of the community when there is little guidance from Qur'an or hadith) must be of great importance.

- The American Muslim must be a Western Muslim, not an Arab Muslim, African Muslim, or Southeast Asian Muslim.

- The West should no longer be considered *dar al harb*, but *dar al shahada*, the land where a Muslim announces his/her faith and testifies to his/her faith.

Recall:

adat, burka, dar al shahada, diaif, huddad, hukh, ibadat, isnad, muamala, mufti, nikah, qadi, sahih, shura, wazir

Reflect:

In Islam almost every human action is law-guided. Construct an imaginary set of laws to be applied to American fast food (McDonald's?) eating.

Respond:

1. What is the foundation(s) of Islamic law?

2. Why would Islamic religion play such a major role in Islamic political thinking?

3. What is the purpose of a *fatwa*? What can it do? Not do?

4. Can you summarize how an Islamic law court works?

5. In what ways is an Islamic law court different from an American one?

6. How can the notions of *ibadat* and *muamala* be related to the Ten Commandments?

7. How are Islamic law and jurisprudence different from U.S. laws and jurisprudence?

8. What do you think of *huddad*?

9. Could a modern society be successfully run by applying Islamic law? What would be its benefits? What would be its shortcomings?

10. Why would an Islamic scholar reject the idea of democracy?

PRAYER AND PREACHING

1. Muslims are to perform *salat* (pray) five times daily. This is dictated in the Five Pillars of Faith. The *salat* ritual is part of *ibadat* (the rituals and practices by which one worships Allah).

    - The five prayer times are *Salatu-l-Fajr* (early morning, around dawn), *Salatu-z-Suhr* (noon), *Salatu-l-Asr* (mid-afternoon), *Salatu l-Maghrib* (sunset), and *Salatu-l-Isha* (evening—any time after an hour and a half past sunset).

    - Some Muslims claim only three prayer sessions a day.

2. From a prayer tower the *ahdan* (the signal to the community that it is prayer time) is called by the *muezzin* (the one who calls the faithful to prayer). In modern times, the call to pray comes most frequently from loud speakers that are broadcasting tape recordings.

    - The first words that the muezzin calls out are *"Allahu Akbar"*—"God is most great." This line (repeated four times is called the *takbir*.

    - Next the muezzin calls out "(I testify that there is) no God but God (or Allah)." These words are called *tahlil*, and they come just before "(I testify that) Mohammed is the messenger of God." And these two phrases together form the *shahada* (the Islamic credo), "There is no god but Allah, and Mohammed is his prophet."

3. A Muslim can pray anywhere, but the *mas'jid* (mosque) is favored. The Friday afternoon prayer service is thought of as special with the *imam* (religious leader) or *mullah* (Qur'anic teacher) or simply a prayer leader providing a homily.

    - In larger mosques, the homily might be delivered from a *minbar* (pulpit).

    - While a Muslim is traveling, prayer is not required.

4. Before entering the mosque, the worshipper must prepare himself or herself. Shoes are removed and shelved and the ablutions (washing) are done following a specific pattern. The feet, arms and face are washed (but only with water and if no water is available sand will be used), and then the mouth, nose, and ears are rinsed.

- These ablutions carry the symbolism of being both clean of dirt and cleaned of sin (hearing or speaking of sinful things).

- Both the washing and prayer sessions are separated by gender. During prayer women are in a curtained-off area or separate room or place.

5. Prayers are lead by a prayer leader (or *imam* or *mullah*), who stands before the *jama'ah* (congregation), facing the same way as the congregants, that is toward Mecca. In the mosque, the direction of Mecca is marked out by the *mihrab* (a niche or indentation in the wall).

- Congregants assemble to say their prayers in orderly rows, one row after another.

- Facing Mecca means facing the Kaaba, the holiest sanctuary in Islam. The Kaaba was built by Adam at the beginning of time and is the earthly counterpart to Allah's throne in heaven.

- The worshipper is face-to-face with Allah. There is no intervening priest, nor are there patron saints, or a savior.

6. First, the worshipper recites the *Fatiha* ("The Opening") which is the first *sura* of the Qur'an and has in its first line the *Bismillah*: "In the name of God (or "Allah") the Compassionate (or "Most Gracious") the Caring" (or "Most Merciful").

- The Muslim in saying the *Fatiha* is in the act of *salat* (pure worship, ritual prayer); he or she is not asking for anything such as a divine blessing or something desired to happen.

- Prayer must come from the heart, from one's innermost being; the mere repeating of words or "going through the motions" is useless. Prayer must come from the heart, from one's innermost being; the mere repeating of words or "going through the motions" is useless. Praying must be a felt, special experience.

- Next, worshippers recite another portion of the Qur'an that they may choose at their own discretion.

- After completing the *Fatiha* and a portion of the Qur'an, then during a prayer session one may ask for a special favor from God.

7. As the prayers are recited, the worshipper moves through a set pattern of movements. He begins in a *qiyam* (standing position) and places his thumbs behind his ears, palms forward, as if listening intently. Next, the hands and arms are brought down, in some traditions to one's sides, and in other traditions the arms are folded right over left across the chest. Then the worshipper bows with hands on knees. Next he kneels, and while kneeling touches his forehead to the floor. This is done twice, and in between each complete bow, he comes back to a sitting position. This movement, almost a complete prostration, is called "*sajdah*" and the sitting position is called *qa'dah*. In the *qa'dah* position the worshipper turns to his right and left and says the greeting *as-salaami-alaykum* (peace on you and Allah's mercy) as a greeting to fellow worshippers (some say it is to the two angels on his shoulders who record good and bed deeds.)

- This movement and prayers are repeated a number of times—two, three, or four cycles depending on which of the five daily prayer sessions one is attending. Each cycle is called a *rak'ah* (literally, "a bowing").

8. The form of the mosque service is based on a variety of *hadith*.

- In different countries the mosque ritual may hold different symbolic meaning for participants. To some it may symbolize community—marking out those included and those outside the community. To others it may symbolize a special closeness to Allah, or a special private conversation between the worshipper and Allah.

9. Local *imams* or "preachers" will provide talks, both formal and informal, on a variety of ethical, theological, legalistic, and historical themes.

- Such themes in ethics as almsgiving, modesty, equality, hypocrisy, adultery, and greed are covered; in Islamic theology miracles, creation, immortality, and polytheism are presented; in terms of legal theory the proper age of worship and ritual impurity are topics; and in history the Battle of Badr and early tribal loyalties might be reviewed.

10. The month of Ramadan (the name of the month is "Ramadan") is a special time. Celebrated during this month is Allah's call to Mohammad to be His prophet to the Arabs and to be the "Seal of Prophets." It was during this month that Gabriel told Mohammed to recite the words of Allah and the first *sura* (chapter of the Qur'an) was delivered. It is a month of spiritual and physical discipline, and a time to do better at spreading love, peace, and reconciliation with enemies.

- Many Muslims will read the entire Qur'an during Ramadan as an act of piety. In the evening they might go to a mosque for *tarawih* (a special extra prayer session).

- Important at this time is the daylight *sawm* (fasting) and prayerful reflection. Eating, drinking, and sex are allowed after dark.

11. *'Id* (or *'Eid*, festival) is rooted in the Arab word meaning "returning at regular intervals." Though there are several important times in the Islamic year, there are two exceptionally important religious festivals. The two festivals are *Eid ul-Adha* (the feast of sacrifice that takes place during the *Hajj*), and the *Eid-ul-Fitr*, the feast that ends the fast at the end of Ramadan.

- *Eid ul-Adha* (Festival of Sacrifice, the "major festival") lasts four days and comes at the end of the Hajj (even for those who have not made the Hajj) on the 10th of Sul Hijja. The holiday commemorates Prophet Ibrahim's (Abraham) willingness to sacrifice his son Ishmael (not Isaac), and Ibrahim's triumph over the temptation of the devil. The celebration is a serious one as it symbolizes every Muslim's submission to Allah. A goat or a lamb is sacrificed by the head of the family, and everyone partakes of the food.

- *Eid-ul-Fitr* [also known as *Sheker Bairam* (Turkish, "sweet festival"), *Eid Ramadan*, and *Eid ul-Sagheer* (the "little/minor festival")] lasts for three days, and it is a day of feasting; remembrance of Allah; and a feeling of closeness to family, ancestors, the *umma* (Muslim community). Especially on this day the poor must be remembered and a special *zakat* (alms) should be delivered to the community's poor or sent to relatives in a foreign country who have little. This holiday comes at the end of Ramadan.

- There are many other important days on the Islamic calendar. 1. *Muharram* is the first month of the Islamic calendar and therefore *Muharram* 1st is New Year's Day. The day commemorates when Mohammad began his *hijira*, and symbolically every Muslim is to "migrate" from the past to the next year, putting old sins behind him or her, and making a clean, fresh start. 2. *Ashura* is the 10th of Muharram, and the day celebrates the creation of the seven heavens and the land and seas; the birth of Adam; the day Nuh (Noah) left the Ark; Ibrahim's birth; the day the Prophet Ayyub (Job) was freed of his travails; the day Allah saved Musa from Pharoah; the day the prophet Isa was born, and the day on which will be the Day of Judgment. [The Shi'ites commemorate the martyrdom of Hussain (Mohammad's grandson) at Karbala on this day (61 A.H.).] 3. *Milad an-Nabi*, which is on the 12th of Rabi'ul-Awwal, is celebrated as the birthday of Mohammad (probably August 20, 570). Though a major holiday in Turkey, some religious jurists and leaders hold that it is idolatry to celebrate Mohammad's birth date. It is a day for special love, blessing, and reverence directed to Mohammad. 4. *Laylat ul-Isra wal-Miraj* is the 27th of Rajab, and it commemorates Mohammad's night journey and ascent to heaven. Mohammad traveled with the angel Gabriel on Buraq, a winged horse, from Mecca to Jerusalem, and then to both Hell and Paradise, and finally up through the heavens to where he was in the presence of Allah. 5. *Laylat ul-Bara'at* is the 14th of Shaban, and it is called the "Night of the Blessing" or "Night of the Decree." It is the night of the full moon before Ramadan. Many devout Muslims will spend the whole night in prayer. Muslims believe that on this night Allah decides who will live and who will die. 6. *Laylat ul-Qadr* is on the 27th of the month of Ramadan, and it is the "Night of Power," the night Mohammad received the first verse of the Qur'an.

12. Sufis represent the mystical side of Islam, and they are found throughout the various Muslim sects, whether Shi'ite, Sunni, Ismaili, or others.

- Sufis say that God is within each of us, and then by employing various meditation techniques they claim that they become one with Allah and all of Reality—claims that other Muslims have at times called heretical. The famous Sufi (and poet) Jalal al-Din Rumi proclaimed the oneness of the universe in wild love poetry.

- Ibn Arabi, the classical Sufi author who wrote *The Meccan Revelations*, *The Essentials of Wisdom*, and *The Interpreter of Dreams*, combined Muslim and Neo-Platonist thought, and then "de-rationalized" the two to make a mystical philosophy. Basing his philosophy on intuitive revelation, he said that the human mind was a (down-graded) emanation of Allah's mind. Like other mystics, he emphasized the oneness of the universe.

- One meditation device is *dihkr/zikr* (the "recollection" of the name of Allah). *Zikr* can be performed either aloud or silently, alone or in a group. In chanting a *zikr* (either aloud or silently) one follows a formula of words glorifying Allah. A rocking movement or even a dance as with the Whirling Dervishes may accompany or be the *zikr*.

- Another meditation practice is the innumerable repetitions of the same word or phrase, through which the chanter seeks complete forgetfulness of self in order to achieve a complete consciousness of Allah. The goal is the symbolic cleansing of the heart of all distractions and the impression on one's heart of the single name of Allah.

- A third meditation device is rehearsing the ninety-nine attributes of Allah while running *tabish* (prayer beads, rosary) through one's fingers. This reciting of attributes is repeated over and over.

- If the chanting is successful, the chanter will feel warmth and agitation, and physical symptoms such as hairs standing on end, spontaneous speaking, laughing, weeping, and visions of light.

Recall:

ahdan, Fatiha, imam, jama'ah, mihrab, minbar, muezzin, mullah, rak'ah, tabish, tahil, takbir, zikr

Reflect:

Compare American holidays or Christian holidays with Muslim ones. Make a listing of the similarities you have found.

Respond:

1. What can be said about the aesthetic and psychological effects on a community of believers hearing the call to prayer?

2. How are the bodily movements made by Muslims in prayer different from Christians (of various denominations) at prayer?

3. What do the bodily movements imply or symbolize?

4. Why would women be separated from men?

5. Why would a religion ask its followers to worship five times daily?

6. Why would one need to wash in a certain way before praying?

7. Approximately five to seven million Muslims live in the U.S. Is Muslim prayer and ritual compatible with contemporary life in the U.S.?

8. How is Muslim prayer and ritual similar to other Western religions?

9. What sort of practices do Sufis believe bring them closer to Allah?

10. Why would some Muslims think that Sufism is a heresy?

SECTION 2

SUPPORT

MATERIALS

TIMELINE OF IMPORTANT EVENTS

476 is the traditionally given date for the fall of the Roman Empire, though in reality the Empire had not only been decaying but also transmuting into something else since 300. The western half of the Empire fell into what is known as the European Dark Ages, while the Eastern half (historians call it the Byzantine Empire), ruled from Constantinople, would survive until 1453. Farther to the east was the Sassanian Empire, another manifestation of centuries of Persian power. The Sassanians and the Romans were at constant warfare at their mutual border.

529   Roman-Byzantine Emperor Justinian and Empress Theodora close the schools of philosophy because many philosophers reject Christianity. Philosophers take their libraries beyond the eastern borders of the Empire.

570   Mohammed is born in Mecca.

610   The first revelation of the Qur'an is delivered to Mohammed.

622/A.H. 1 Mohammed leaves Mecca for Medina. This "migration" or "breaking of old ties" marks the formal beginning of the Muslim calendar and the beginning of formal Islam. (A.H. as in Latin *anno hegirae*, year of the migration)

624   Mohammed leads ghazi raids on Meccan camel caravans. Three major conflicts occur between the Meccans and Medinans.

625   Mohammed expels the Jewish tribes from Medina.

630   The Meccans capitulate to Mohammed and his army. No blood is shed.

632   Mohammed dies. Abu Bakr becomes caliph. Abu Bakr and the next three caliphs—Umar, Uthman, and Ali—are known as the *Rashidun*, the Rightly Guided Ones.

638   Muslim armies conquer Jerusalem; they then continue on to Damascus.

641   The Sassanians to the northeast and the Egyptians to the west fall to Muslim armies.

661   Ali is murdered by Kharajite dissenters, and Muawiyah declares himself the fifth caliph. This begins the Umayyad dynasty. His capital is Damascus.

680   Husain, Ali's son is killed at Karbala. His followers call themselves the *Shiah i Ali* (the Followers of Ali)—the Shi'ites.

691   The Dome of the Rock is built in Jerusalem. One tradition has it that the structure commemorates the spot where Mohammed stepped off the Earth onto Baraq for a flight to the seventh heaven.

712   The Straits of Gibraltar are crossed and three-quarters of Spain is conquered by Muslim armies.

732   Charles Martel stops Muslim advances at Poitiers.

749   The Abbasids overthrow the Umayyads.

800 The "Golden Age" in Islam begins; it is a period of great intellectual developments, scientific progress, and technological advances.

835   Caliph Ma'mun opens the Bayt al Hikma, a school of higher learning in Damascus. Tension between two groups of philosopher-theologians, the Mu'tazilites and the Ash'arites, leads to suppression of the Ash'arites.

1000   The European Dark Ages begin to lighten. Historians call the next three hundred or so years the High Middle Ages. In Spain the Reconquista begins.

1071   At the Battle of Manzikurt in Anatolia (modern Turkey) Muslim Seljuk Turk armies rout Byzantine armies. Shortly, most of Anatolia will fall to Turkish armies.

1094   Eastern Orthodox Christian Byzantine Emperor Alexius Commenus I sends a plea for help against the Turks to the Roman Catholic Church of western Europe. Pope Urban announces the First Crusade the following year.

1099   The Crusaders take Jerusalem. They slaughter Muslims, Christians, and Jews living in Jerusalem.

1187   At the battle of Hittin, Sal al-din defeats the Crusaders and captures Jerusalem.

1220   Mongol raiding begins on the eastern lands of *Dar al Islam*.

1350   The Renaissance begins in Florence, Italy.

1400   Modern scholars cite this date as the end of Islam's "Golden Age".

1453   Memed II captures Constantinople. The city becomes the capital of the Ottoman Empire which stretches from Vienna across the Middle East and across North Africa. Christian Greek scholars, taking precious manuscripts with them, leave Constantinople for Italy.

1492   The Reyes Catholicos drive out the last Muslim rulers in Spain. The Inquisition drives out Muslims and Jews. Christopher Columbus discovers for Europeans a new continent.

1510   Ismail establishes the Safavid Empire in the area now called Iraq and Iran.

1513   Portuguese sailors reach China.

1560   Under Emperor Akbar the Mughal Empire reaches the height of power and culture.

1600   The Age of Reason begins in Europe. Philosophers and scientists of the caliber of Bacon, Galileo, Descartes, Hobbes, Gassendi, Locke, Leibniz, and Newton will populate western Europe. Revolutionary developments in science, technology, political philosophy, religion, and social organization are given no notice beyond Europe.

1601   The Dutch sail into Indonesia and set up trading colonies. This area will soon be known to Europeans as the Dutch East Indies.

1699   The Treaty of Carlowicz is viewed as a victory by the European powers and as a serious defeat for the Ottoman Empire. The long slide to the Empire's end begins here.

1774   The Crimea is taken over by the Russians with the defeat of Ottoman forces.

1776   America's Declaration of Independence is written.

1789   The French Revolution topples the monarchy and *ancien régime*.

1798   Napoleon takes Egypt.

1814   Russia takes the Caucasus from the Ottomans.

1839   The British, on their way to realizing the slogan, "The sun never sets on the British Empire," seize control of Aden at the tip of Arabia.

1861   The French assume control over Lebanon.

1897   The first Zionist conference asks for a Jewish homeland in the Ottoman province of Palestine.

1914   World War I breaks out in Europe with the assassination of Archduke Ferdinand in Sarajevo. Sarajevo had been a fortified Ottoman town, then part of the Austro-Hungarian Empire, and then Yugoslavia. As in the rest of the Balkans, its population was mainly Slavs with a religious mix of Roman Catholics, Greek Orthodox, Sunni and Shi'ite Muslims, and Jews.

1919   World War I ends. The League of Nations slices up the defunct Ottoman Empire into nation-states on a European model. Borders are often "lines drawn in the sand."

1921   The Republic of Turkey headed by Mustafa Kemal (Ataturk) is established out of the ruins of the old Ottoman Empire.

1922   Egypt receives a large measure of independence from the British government.

1929   The Great Depression strikes Western nations. With financial disaster as a major cause, fascism and racism combine in political platforms in several nations.

1932   The House of Saudi forms an independent Saudi Arabia.

1939   World War II breaks out with the German invasion of Poland. In the next few years, approximately 63,000,000 people will die from hostilities and the *Shoah* in Europe will claim 6,000,000 Jews.

1945   World War II ends with the dropping of two atomic bombs on Japan.

1948   The United Nations creates the state of Israel. Pakistan is partitioned from India. It is Muslim while India is Hindu.

1952   King Faruk is forced out of Egypt and Jamal al-Nasser takes power. The Muslim Brotherhood is suppressed.

1954   The Algerian civil war begins.

1967   The Six Day War between Israel and Arab states. The Arab states suffer a shocking defeat.

1979   Israeli Prime Minister Menachem Begin and Egyptian President Anwar El Sadat sign the Egypt-Israel Peace Treaty. The Iranian Revolution forces out the Shah who is replaced by Shi'ite cleric Ayatollah Khomeini. Iran becomes the first modern Islamic Republic.

1980-1988 The Iran-Iraq war sees the death of over 500,000 soldiers and civilians in a conflict that changed no national borders nor gained any strategic political advantages. Iran sends to the front *basijs*—untrained and poorly armed child and teenage soldiers in human waves to counter the Iraqi offensives. The war is fought over territory, the promise of oil and its revenues, and because of Sunni-Shi'ite hatreds.

1989   Salman Rushdie, the author of *Satanic Verses*, is condemned to death in a fatwa issued by Ayatollah Ruhollah Khomeni. Khomeni claims that Rushdie has blasphemed against the Islamic faith. Naguib Mahfouz, an Egyptian novelist and winner of the Nobel Prize for Literature, joins other intellectuals in denouncing the fatwa. A few years later Mahfouz himself is almost killed by Muslim extremists.

1990   The (Persian) Gulf War begins when Iraq, under Saddam Hussein, invades Kuwait. Within months, a coalition of forces eject Saddam's forces and destroy most of his military. Though Israel is attacked by Scud missiles, at the request of western powers it does not retaliate—Arab coalition members would have to back out if it were thought by the Arab masses that they were fighting on the same side as Israel.

1992   Civil war breaks out in Yugoslavia. The phrase "ethnic cleansing" (Muslims are forced to leave their homes or murdered) appears in news reports.

1994   The Treaty of Peace between the State of Israel and the Hashemite Kingdom of Jordan is signed.

2001   On September 11, terrorists murder close to 3,000 people in New York's World Trade Towers by flying two commercial jets into the building. The US sends troops into Afghanistan to destroy al Qaeda, the group that claimed responsibility for the World Trade Towers disaster. The warfare broadens into America's desire to root out al Qaeda's supporters, the Taliban, a *salafiist* organization which controls much of Afghanistan.

2005   The Jyllands-Posten, a Danish newspaper, publishes unflattering cartoons of Mohammed. Many Muslims around the world are furious.

2007   Israel destroys Syria's nuclear reactor. Iran proceeds with its nuclear program.

2010   Western nations continue to experience terrorist attacks sponsored by radical religious groups.

2011   Various Arab states see people rising up to overthrow what they view as repressive governments. Tunisia is first, followed by Egypt, Yemen, Libya, Bahrain, and Syria. Newscasters title the wave of uprisings the "Arab Spring."

2012 C.E. (A.D.) on the Gregorian calendar is the year A.H. **1434.**

The Islamic calendar, properly known as the Hijri/Hijiri calendar, begins its yearly dating with A.H. 1, the year that Mohammed left Mecca and "migrated" to Yatrib/Medina. A.H. 1 would be 622 C.E. (A.D.) on the standard Western Gregorian calendar. A. H. is *Anno Hegirae* (Latin) or "Year of the *Hijira*".

Umar ibn Al-Khattab, Islam's second caliph, recognized the need for an Arab Muslim calendar, and so developed one based on the appearances of the "new" moon, a lunar calendar of twelve months each month having either 29 or 30 days. This means that 354 days make up a year. Lunar-based months are not synchronized with the seasons (which result from the Earth's movement about the sun) as is a solar-based calendar with its 365.25 days (the time it takes for the Earth to travel about the sun). Why Umar chose a lunar-based calendar is uncertain, but there are at least two possible explanations. First, many other Middle Eastern communities had such calendars. Second, and maybe more importantly, the Qur'an in 10:5 appears to instruct that time should be measured by the moon.

Each of the Hijri calendar's twelve months begins at the sighting of the new moon. The names of the months and important dates are as follows:

- Muharram (Muharram 1 is New Year's Day. Muharran 10 is Day of Ashura, and on this day Sunnis celebrate Moses's victory over the Pharoah while Shi'ites commemorate the death of Hussein ibn Ali at the Battle of Karbala.)

- Safar

- Rabi'I

- Rabi'll

- Jumada I

- Jumada II

- Rajab   (Raja 27, Laylat ul Isra/Miraj (Night of The Mirage), celebrates Mohammed's Night Journey to the seventh heaven.)

- Sha'aban

- Ramadan [Ramadan 1 is the first day of the Ramadan fast. Laylat al Qadr (Night of Power) falls some time during the last ten days of Ramadan, and it notes the first deliverance of the Qur'an.]

- Shawwal [Eid al Fit (Festival of Breaking the Fast of Ramadan) falls on Shawwal 1.]

- Dhu al Qa'dah

- Dhu al Hijjah [This is the month for the Hajj—days 8th through 13th. On the 9th of Dhu al Hijjah is Eid al Adha (Festival of Sacrifice) which commemorates Abraham's willingness to sacrifice Ishmael.]

- The seven days of the week:

- Yaum (day) al Ahad [Day First (Sunday)]

- ...al Ithnayn (Day Second)

- …Thalatha (Day Third)
- …Arba'a (Day Fourth)
- …Khamis (Day Fifth)
- …Jumu'a [Day of Gathering (Friday), and so the importance of Friday afternoon prayers]
- …Sabt (Sabbath)

Before the adoption of Umar's dating system, a year would be named by an important event which took place during that year. Hence, the Year of the Elephant named a year when a great battle was fought between Meccans and elephant-deploying Yemenites. Many scholars have concluded that that year was 570 C.E., and since the Hijri calendar only dates forward from A.H. 1, Mohammed's birth date for Muslims is the Year of the Elephant. As to other years before A.H.1, this time is known as the *jahiliya* (confusion/era of confusion), and so it is considered unimportant to provide a specific dating system.

FACT SHEET NATION-STATES IN DAR AL ISLAM

Afghanistan

Islamic Republic of Afghanistan: Independence 1919, Islamic republic, governed by Western-style civil law and *Shari'a*, numerous political parties, constitution with executive, bicameral legislature, and judicial branches, approximate population 28,400,000, ethnic identity Pashtun 42%, Tajik 27%, Hazara 9%, Uzbek 9%, Sunni Muslim 80%, Shi'ite 19%.

- Concerns: Political instability, ethnic/tribal rivalries, al Qaeda, Taliban salafiism.

Algeria

Peoples Democratic Republic of Algeria: Independence 1962, republic, governed by *Shari'a* law and French legal codes, numerous political parties, parliament (bicameral: Council of the Nation and National People's Assembly), approximate population 34,000,000, Berber ethnic identity, 99% Sunni Muslim.

- Concerns: Civil strife—Berbers want independence from Arab elite and culture.

Egypt

Arab Republic of Egypt: Independence 1922 (republic declared 1953, complete British withdrawal 1956), republic, governed by *Shari'a* and Napoleonic codes, advisory to the chief of state system [bicameral: *Majlis al Shura* (Advisory Council) and *Majlis al Sha'b* (People's Assembly)], approximate population 79,000,000, Egyptian ethnic identity, 90% Sunni Muslim, 9% Coptic, 1% Christian.

- Concerns: Tensions between the Muslim Brotherhood and the military establishment. Relations with Coptic population.

Indonesia

Republic of Indonesia: Independence 1945 (declared 1945, recognized by Netherlands 1949), republic, governed by Roman-Dutch legal system, numerous political parties, executive, legislative, and judicial government branches, approximate population 240,000,000, Indonesian ethnic identity, Sunni Muslim 86%, Protestant 6%, Roman Catholic 3%, Hindu 2%, other 3 to 4%.

- Concerns: Socio-political demands by Muslims for *Shari'a*-style government and law.

Iran

Islamic Republic of Iran: Independence 1979 (Persia first unified as an empire in 625 B.C.E., theocracy-republic, governed by *Shari'a* law, semi-legal political parties, unicameral *Majles e Shura ye Eslami* (Consultative Assembly), approximate population 66,500,000, 51% Persian ethnic identity, 24% Azeri, Kurd 7%, other 18%, 89% Shi'ite, 9% Sunni.

- Concerns: Dealing with Western and Saudi hostility toward Iran.

Iraq

Republic of Iraq: Independence 1932 (2004 authority transferred to Coalition Provisional Authority; constitution ratified 2005, subject to further review), republic, governed by Shari'a law and European civil codes, numerous political parties, approximate population 29,000,000 Shi'ite 60-65%, Sunni 32-37%, Christian or other 3%.

- Concerns: The civil unrest between Shi'ite and Sunni; establishment of a secure government.

Jordan

Hashemite Kingdom of Jordan: Independence 1946, constitutional monarchy, governed by *Shari'a* law and French legal codes, numerous political parties, the National Assembly is the *Majlis al Umma* [Majlis al Ayan (the Senate or House of Notables), Majlis al Nuwaab (House of Representatives or Chamber of Deputies)] ,approximate population 6,300,000, 92% Sunni Muslim.

- Concerns: The Influx of Iraqis; balancing relations with Arab states and Israel.

Lebanon

Lebanese Republic: Independence 1943, republic, governed by a mix of Ottoman law, canon law, Napoleonic code, and civil law, numerous political parties, unicameral Majlis al Nuwab (National Assembly), approximate population 4,000,000, 17 recognized religious sects with 60% Muslim (Shia, Sunni, Druze, Isma'lite, Alawite, Nusayri), 39% Christain (Marionite, Greek Orthodox, Milkite, Armenian Orthodox, Syrian Catholic, etc.).

- Concerns: Fractured socio-political national identity.

Pakistan

Islamic Republic of Pakistan: Independence 1947 (partition from India), governed by English common law with adjustments for Pakistan's Islamic traditions, federal republic (constitution suspended and restored numerous times in past 60 years), numerous political parties, approximate population 174,000,000, a variety of ethnic groups including Punjabi 44.5%, Pashtun/Pathan 15.5%, Sindhi 14%, Sariaki 8.3%, Muhajirs 7.5%, Balochi 3.5%, religions Sunni 75%, Shi'ite 20%, other 5%.

- Concerns: Government political instability; Taliban and Deobondi salafiism, tribal law, tensions with India.

Saudi Arabia

Kingdom of Saudi Arabia: Independence 1932, monarchy, governed by *Shari'a* law with some secular codes, no political parties, *Majlis al Shura* (consultative council of 150 members), approximate population 28,600,000, 100% Sunni Wahabism Muslim.

- Concerns: Oil, distrust of Shi'ite Iran, Mecca.

Syria

Syrian Arab Republic: Independence 1946, republic directed by an authoritarian military regime, governed by French and Ottoman legal codes with a family court system run by *Shari'a*, numerous political parties (some legal, some outlawed), *Majlis al Shaab* (unicameral People's Council), approximate population 21,700,000, Arabs (90%), Kurds, Armenians, Sunni Muslim, Christian.

- Concerns: Relations with Israel (Israeli occupies Golan Heights since 1973 war), involvement with Lebanon, and as of 2012, a civil war.

Turkey

Republic of Turkey: Independence 1923, republican parliamentary democracy, legal system based on various European legal systems, numerous political parties, approximate population 77,000,000, ethnic diversity Turkish 70-75%, Kurd 18%, 99% Sunni.

- Concerns: Entrance into the European Common Market, salafiism.

CLASSIFYING ISLAMIC MOVEMENTS

In attempting to categorize the various contemporary Islamic movements and ideologies scholars apply a variety of labels. The labels could roughly be arranged from the socio-political left to right as:

- Radical Left (as in Communist)
- Liberal (or Progressive or Socialist)
- Modernist (attempting to blend Islam with Western culture)
- Traditionalist (or Conservative)
- Fundamentalist (attempting to adhere to pre-9th century Islam)
- Islamist (complete rejection of Western culture).

Yes, some of these distinctions are not as clear as one might hope, but used guardedly they could be helpful. Consider some Islamic movement or ideology such as the Wahabis, Taliban, or Salafiism, and determine the proper label by considering the most obvious way we associate the following characteristics with such a movement or ideology. Note that some of the characteristics overlap and there may be other characteristics that you think should be added. Does the movement advocate any of the following:

1.   Democratic participation in politics?
2.   Wearing the veil, hajab, or burka?
3.   An Islamic state?
4.   A secular state?
5.   An Islamicate state?
6.   A theocracy?
7.   The adoption of secular law?
8.   Islamic law/*Shari'a*?
9.   A combination of secular and Islamic law/*Shari'a*?
10.   Women's active role in society and government?
11.   The use of modern technologies?
12.   A resistance to Western culture?
13.   A return to the period of the Rashidun (Islam's first century)?
14.   Social justice for all?
15.   Islamic schools?
16.   Secular universities?

17. Specialized Islamic dress codes for males?

18. _____?*

19. _____?

20. _____?

For example: Wahabis advocate 2, 3, 6, 8, 12, 15, and 17. One might see such characteristics as Traditionalist or Fundamentalist, but certainly not Progressive, Liberal, Modernist, or Moderate.

*Terrorism has become a world concern, and its sources are various. Does the movement advocate:

a. Religious fundamentalism terrorism?

b. State-sponsored terrorism?

c. Political revolutionary terrorism?

d. Single-issue terrorism?

BOOK REPORT LIST

(Note: The books here listed would be good choices for book reports. This listing contains fiction and non-fiction as well as both prose and poetry.)

Among the Believers: An Islamic Journey. V.S. Naipal. New York: Random House (Vintage Books), 1982. ISBN 0-394-71195-5 (paperback)

A Peace to End All Peace. David Fromkin. New York: Henry Holt and Co. (An Owl Book), 2001. ISBN 0-8050-6884-8 (hardcover)

A Season in Bethlehem: Unholy War in a Sacred Place. Joshua Hammer. New York: Simon and Schuster (Free Press), 2003.   ISBN 0-7432-5604-2 (paperback)

A Thousand Splendid Suns. Khaled Hosseini. New York: Riverhead Trade (reprint edition), 2008. ISBN 10-159448385X (paperback)

Battle for God, The. Karen Armstrong. New York: Ballatine Books, 2001. ISBN 0-345-39169-1 (paperback)

Bed of Red Flowers, A. Nelofer Pazira. New York: Free Press, 2005. ISBN-10 0743281331 (paperback)

Behind the Veil in Arabia: Women in Oman. Unni Wikan. Chicago: University of Chicago Press, 1982. ISBN 0-226-89683-8 (paperback)

Beyond Belief: Islamic Excursions Among the Converted People. V.S. Naipal. New York: Vintage Books, 1999. ISBN-10 0375706488 (paperback)

Cairo House, The. Samia Serageldin. Syracuse: Syracuse University Press, 2003. ISBN-10 0815607938. (paperback)

Caravan of Dreams. Idries Shah. London: Octagon Press, 1995. ISBN 0-863040-43-8 (paperback)

Conference of Birds, The. Farid Ud-Din Attar. Translated by Darbandi and Davis. New York: Penguin Books, 1984.   ISBN 0-14-044434-3 (paperback)

Crusades Through Arab Eyes, The. Amin Maalouf. New York: Shocken Books, 1989. ISBN-10 0805208984 (paperback)

End of Days, The: Fundamentalism and the Struggle for the Temple Mount. Gershon Gorenberg. New York: Oxford University Press, 2000. ISBN 0-19-515205-0 (paperback)

Following Mohammad: Rethinking Islam in the Contemporary World. Carl W. Ernst. Chapel Hill: University of North Carolina Press, 2003. ISBN 0-8078-2837-8 (hardbound)

Getting God's Ear. Eleanor Abdella Doumato. New York: Columbia University Press, 2000.   ISBN-10 0231116675 (paperback)

Hadj, The. Michael Wolfe. New York: Grove Press, 1993. ISBN 0-8021-3586-2 (paperback)

Honor Lost: Love and Death in Modern Day Jordan. Norma Khouri. New York: Washington Square Press, 2003.   ISBN 0-7434-4879-0 (paperback)

Infidels: *A History of the Conflict between Christendom and Islam.* Andrew Wheatcraft. New York: Random House, 2005. ISBN-10 0812972392

Inside the Kingdom: My Life in Saudi Arabia. Carmen Bin Laden. New York: Grand Central Publishing, 2005. ISBN-10 0446694886 (paperbook)

Islam and Democracy: *Fear of the Modern World.* Fatema Mernissi. Translated by Mary Jo Lakeland. Cambridge, MA: Perseus Publishing, 2002. ISBN 0-7382-0745-4 (paperback)

Islam and the Bible: Why Two Faiths Collide. David Goodmann. Chicago: Moody Publishers, 2004. ISBN 0-8024-1017-0 (paperback)

Islam and the Challenge of Democracy. Khaled Abou El Fadl. Princeton: Princeton University Press (A Boston Review Book), 2004. ISBN 0-691-11938-4 (paperback)

Islam Today: A Short Introduction to the Muslim World. Akbar S. Ahmed. New York: I.B. Tauris Publishers, 2001. ISBN 1-86064-257-8 (paperback)

Jesus and Mohammad: The Parallel Sayings. Edited by Joey Green. Berkeley: Seastone, 2003. ISBN 1-56975-326-1 (paperback)

Jinnah, Pakistan and Islamic Identity: The Search for Saladin. Akbar S. Ahmed. New York: Routledge, 2002. ISBN 0-415-14966-5 (paperback)

Kite Runner, The. Khaled Hosseini. New York: Penguin, 2003. ISBN 1-57322-245-3 (paperback)

Lipstick Jihad. Azadeh Moaveni. New York: Public Affairs, 2006. ISBN-10 1586483781 (paperback)

Lords of the Horizon: A History of the Ottoman Empire. Jason Goodwin. New York: Henry Holt and Co. (Picador), 1998. ISBN 0-312-42066-8 (paperback)

Moorish Spain. Richard Fletcher. Berkeley: University of California Press, 2006. ISBN 0-520-08496-9 (paperback)

Muslim Politics. Dale F. Eickelman and James Piscatori. Princeton: Princeton University Press, 1996. ISBN 0-691-00870-1 (paperback)

My Forbidden Face, Growing Up Under the Taliban: A Young Girl's Story. Latifa. New York: Miramax, 2003. ISBN-10 1401359256 (paperback)

Nine Parts of Desire: *The Hidden World of Islamic Women.* Geraldine Brooks. New York: Anchor Books, 1995. ISBN-10 0385475772 (paperback)

Out of Place: A Memoir. Edward W. Said. New York: Random House (Vintage Books), 1999. ISBN 0-679-73067-2 (paperback)

Passion for Islam: Shaping the Modern Middle East — The Egyptian Experience. Caryle Murphy. New York: Scribner (A Lisa Drew Book), 2002. ISBN 0-7434-4879-0 (paperback)

Persepolis: The Story of a Childhood. Marjane Satrapi. New York: Pantheon, 2004. ISBN 037571457X (paperback)

Price of Honor. Jan Goodwin. New York: Plumb (revised edition), 2002. ISBN-10 0452283779. (paperback)

Reading Lolita in Tehran: A Memoir in Books. Azar Nafisi. New York: Random House (Trade Paperbacks Edition), 2004. ISBN 0-8129-7106-X (papeback)

Sand Child, The. Tahar Jelloun. Baltimore: Johns Hopkins, 2000. ISBN-10 0801864402 (paperback)

Satanic Verses, The. Salman Rushdie. New York: Random House Trade Paperbacks, 2008 (original date 1988). ISBN-10 0812976711 (paperback)

Shade of the Swords, The. M.J. Akbar. Routledge (revised edition). 2003. ISBN-10 0415328144 (paperback)

Teachings of Rumi. Andrew Harvey. Boston: Shambhala, 1999. ISBN 1570623465 (paperback)

Three Cups of Tea, Greg Mortenson and David Relin. New York: Viking Press, March 2006. ISBN-10 0143038257 (paperback)

Trouble with Islam, The. Irshad Manji. New York: St. Martin's Press, 2002. ISBN-10 1840188375 (paperback)

Warriors of God: Richard the Lionheart and Saladin in the Third Crusade. James Reston, Jr. New York: Random House, 2002. ISBN 0-385-49562-5) (paperback)

What Went Wrong? The Clash Between Islam and Modernity in the Middle East. Bernard Lewis. New York: HarperCollins (Perennial), 2003. ISBN 0-06-051605-4 (paperback)

Why I Am a Muslim: An American Odyssey. Asma Gull Hasan. London: HarperCollins (Element), 2004. ISBN 0-00-7175337 (hardbound)

Wisdom of Idiots. Idries Shah. London: Octagon Press, 1996. ISBN 0-863040-46-2 (paperback)

Women and Gender in Islam: Historical Roots of a Modern Debate. Leila Ahmed. New Haven: Yale University Press, 1993. ISBN 0300055838　　　　(paperback)

Women of Deh Koh: Lives in an Iranian Village. Erika Friedl. New York: Penguin Books, 1991. ISBN 0-1401-4993-7 (paperback)

Zoya's Story: An Afghan Women's Struggle for Freedom. Zoya, John Fullain, Rita Cristofari. New York: Harper Collins, 2002. ISBN 0-06-009782.5 (paperback)

CINEMA VIEWING LIST

(Note: The films here listed would be good choices for film reviews. These selections should be easily located at local rental stores. The reviews were taken from the covers of the videos.)

Afghan Star

"After thirty years of war and Taliban rule, pop Idol has come to Afghanistan. Millions are watching the TV series 'Afghan Star' and voting for their favorite singers by mobile phone. This timely film follows the dramatic stories of four contestants as they risk all to become the nation's favorite singer. But will they attain the freedom they hope for in this vulnerable and traditional nation?" Unrated. 1hr 27 min, 2009.

Ali Baba and the 40 *Thieves*

"Ali Baba accidentally discovers the magic cave where Abdul and his band of 40 thieves hide their ill-gotten treasure. He takes enough gold to buy the beautiful slave girl Morgaine from his master Cassim to be his wife. However, Cassim and Abdul have plans for Ali on his wedding night." Unrated (comedy), 1 hr 32 min, 1950s.

Battle of Algiers

"Shot on location, and starring actual FLN rebels, *Battle of Algiers* is one of the most realistic films of all times. Initially banned by the French government, it quickly won wide acclaim; an Academy Award nomination for the Best Foreign Film and garnering 11 international awards.

"Struggling to rid their country of French colonialism, Ali La Pointe and his terrorist group paint the streets of the Casbah red with the blood of their enemies. Children shoot soldiers at point blank range. Women plant bombs in cafes. Soon the entire Arab population builds to a mad fervor. French Colonel Phillipe Mathieu, a highly decorated officer, is called upon to quash the uprising. But Algiers is on fire and the battle has just begun." Unrated, 2hrs 5 mins, 1966.

The Boy from Lebanon

"In a story ripped from today's headlines, terrorists recruit Djilali, a Lebanese orphan. They teach him to shoot, to fight, to hate, and to be a soldier. When he goes to Paris to assassinate the French President, he meets Karim, a boy from the poor, Arab section of the city, being used unwittingly to help Djilali blend in. Karim knows nothing of terrorism. His interests are those of a boy his age: rap music, skateboarding, cheeseburgers and a crush on a 16-year-old classmate. The boys become close, vowing to remain friends 'for better or worse.' But eventually Djilali must choose between his mission and the life of his friend. Shot in a gritty, pseudo-documentary style, *The Boy from Lebanon* is a brutal portrait of the semantics of war, terror and duty." Unrated, 1 hr 30 min, 1993.

Deserted Station

"In this lyrical and intimately nuanced story conceived by Abbas Kiarostami, a photographer and his young wife are stranded in a remote village after their car breaks down. The only adult inhabitant leaves with the photographer to find help, while the woman takes over the duties of teaching the village children—whose parents are nowhere to be found." Unrated. 1 hr 28 min, date?

The Flying Camel

"A charming comic escapade about a Jewish professor and an Arab garbage collector who embark on an exciting adventure in pursuit of their uncommon interests. The comedy escalates when a young nun encounters the unlikely duo and joins them in a madcap journey through a wild landscape of wit and imagination. A lilting allegory etched against the backdrop of modern Tel Aviv, The Flying Camel is a delightful celebration of the differences that distinguish us and the enduring friendships that emerge when we accept them." Unrated (comedy) 1 hr 32 min, 1995.

Gabbeh

"A folkloric carpet (Gabbeh), picturing a man and a woman riding away on horseback is the prized possession of a nomadic elderly couple. When they sit to wash it on the bank of a creek, a beautiful young women suddenly emerges from the carpet to join them. Once held hostage by the endless restraints of the family that fashioned the carpet, she reveals the secret of the carpet lies within the mysterious black-clad rider on the white horse. Month after month, season after season, he had followed her family from afar, always present, always waiting, howling to her songs of love—longing for her to run away with him." Unrated (fantasy) 1 hr 15 min, 1996.

Halfaouine: Boy of the Terraces

"Set against the sensual, exotic backdrop of modern Tunisia, renowned Arab critic-turned-film-maker Ferid Boughedir's Halfaouine: Boy of the Terraces is a bittersweet portrait of a boy's sexual awakening.

"A sensitive, comical look at the difficulty of growing up under the puritanical codes of Islam, Boughedir's film is also a rich, vibrant portrait of the Arab neighborhood of Halfaouine, with its array of colorful and eccentric citizenry from whom Noura learns the complicated often hypocritical ways of adulthood." Unrated (extensive female nudity) 1 hr 38 min, 1990.

Iron Island

"Moored a few hundred yards off the Persian coast, a derelict oil tanker has become the thriving home for cast-off members of Iran's Sunni-Arab minority. 'As long as I am with you,' says Captain Nemat, proud patriarch of the Iron Island's floating shanty-town, 'you shouldn't worry about a thing.' But when the ship's owners announce they intend to sell Nemat's fiefdom for scrap, and the ad hoc community's on-board teacher discovers that the ship is slowly sinking, the captain must provide his people with a future, while preserving the peace and upholding the law in the present." Unrated, 1 hr 30min, 2005.

Kandahar

"Nafas, an Afghan-born Canadian journalist, returns to her homeland in a desperate attempt to reach her sister. [Nafas' sister] overcome with grief after being injured by a landmine and her despair over the Taliban's systematic oppression of women, she has vowed that she will commit suicide at the time of the next solar eclipse, only three days away.

"Clothed in the traditional head-to-toe burka, and posing as a subservient wife, Nafas' odyssey takes her across a dramatic desert and landscape, when she encounters bandits, corpse-robbers, marooned exiles, overwhelmed Red Cross workers, hordes of land-mine victims, and finally a wedding procession that brings her within eyeshot of Kandahar." Unrated (shocking scenes), 1 hr 25 min, 2001/2003.

The Kite Runner

"As young boys, Amir and Hassan were inseparable friends, until one fateful act tore them apart. Years later, Amir will embark on a dangerous quest to right the wrongs of the past-and redeem himself in ways he never expected by displaying the ultimate in courage and devotion to his friend." PG-13, 2hrs 7min, 2007.

Marooned in Iraq

"During the Iran-Iraq war, an aging Iranian-Kurd musician hears that his wife, a singer with a magical voice who deserted him for his best friend and fled to Iraq, is in trouble. He cons his two sons into accompanying him on the search for her, and they embark on an adventure filled with music, romance and danger. Acclaimed Iranian director Bahman Ghobadi's (A *Time for Drunken Horses)* award-winning film uses humor and wit to dramatize the plight of Kurdish people." Unrated. 1 hr 37min, 2003(?).

Osama

"After the brutal Taliban regime bans women from working and forbids them to leave their homes without a male escort, a 12-year-old girl and her mother find themselves on the brink of starvation. With nowhere left to turn, the mother disguises her daughter as a boy. Now called "Osama," the young girl embarks on a terrifying and confusing journey, as she tries to keep the Taliban from discovering her true identity." PG-13, 1 hr 23min, 2003.

Takva

"Muharrem (Erkan Can) lives a solitary existence, strictly adhering to the most severe Islamic doctrines. To his surprise, a religious leader hires him as a rent collector, where he is given Western-style suits, a cell phone, and a car with a driver. Thrown suddenly into the modern world, the naive Muharrem is exposed to temptations and hypocrisies, causing his fear of God to eat away at his senses, and threaten his sanity." Unrated, 1 hr 36min, 2006.

Turtles Can Fly

"On the Iraqi-Turkish border, enterprising 13-year-old 'Satellite' is the de facto leader of a Kurdish village, thanks to his ability to install satellite dishes and translate news of the impending US invasion. Organizing fellow orphans into landmine-collection teams so that they can eke out a living, he is all business... until the arrival of a clairvoyant boy and his quiet, beautiful sister." PG13 1hr 37 min, 2005.

The Yacoubian Building

"An eye-catching construction, the Yacoubian Building in Cairo was long regarded as the last word in comfort and elegance. Nowadays the veneer has cracked and the shine has dulled to reveal the truth underneath the façade. Though interwoven stories of a number of the residents, the film paints a portrait of corruption, fundamentalism, prostitution, homosexuality, and drugs in central Cairo and creates a vibrant but socially critical picture of contemporary Egypt." Unrated, 2hr 40min. 2006.

TEXTBOOK

INTERNET, CD, DVD, AND READINGS LIST

[NOTE: Unless otherwise cited, all Qur'an readings are from *The Meaning of the Holy Qur'an*, by Abdullah Yusuf Ali. Amana Publications, or *Saheeh International Qur'an* (www.saheehinternational.com/qurantranslation).]

ART AND ARCHITECTURE: www.youtube.com Paradise Found: Islamic Architecture and Art, in 10 parts, each approx. 10 min)

HUMOR: www.youtube.com Hilarious Arab Peoples;

www.youtube.com Arab-American Comedian-Arab Men Checking Out Women

www.youtube.com Arab American Comedian-Arab Pick Up Lines

MAP: www.youtube.com Google Earth program

MUSIC: www.youtube.com nasheed-anwarul Islam

OVERVIEW: www.youtube.com Islam: Empire of Faith. PBS Documentary (in 4 parts, each approx. 55 min)

POPULAR CULTURE: www.youtube.com Arab/Arabic Beauty in the Middle East

www.youtube.com Afghan Beauties, Iranian Beauties, and Indian Beauties

www.youtube.com Top Handsome Arab Men Alive

www.youtube.com Persian Male Models and Celebrities

www.youtube.com SHAAM- Mercy Like the Rain

www.youtube.com Reel Bad Arabs How Hollywood Vilifies A People (in 5 parts, each between approx. 5 and 10 min)

www.youtube.com Spike Jones & His City Slickers-"The Sheik of Araby"-Original "video"

LECTURE ONE: OVERVIEW

Approaching the Koran, p. 150 for interpretation, explanation p. 151; p. 217 for CD track listing, track 1

www.youtube.com Sheikh Sudais Reciting Surah Al-Fatiha

REFLECT: On Google Earth or www.googlemaps.com

LECTURE TWO: ISLAM: A RELIGION AND A WAY OF LIFE

Qur'an 3:101

Qur'an 3:102

Qur'an 3:84

Islam and the West, p. 181

REFLECT: www.youtube.com *"shahada"*

LECTURE THREE: QUR'AN

www.youtube.com "Amazing Quran Girl Khadija Birhoon Islam Quran child kid"

Qur'an 17:88

The Koran: A Very Short Introduction, p. 113

A Reader on Classical Islam, p. 172

The Koran: A Very Short Introduction, p. 119

Qur'an 3:42.

Qur'an 2:253

Qur'an 5:110

www.youtube.com "Hijab Girls-Bismillah by Yusuf Islam"

From *sura* two *al-Baqara*, The Cow. Charity: 2:215, 2:270, 2:271. Gambling and drinking: 2:219. War: 2:216, 2:217, 2:244; Women (marriage) 2:221; Women (sexual intercourse) 2:223.

tafsir issues regarding religion: Qur'an 2:256, 3:85, 3:67

The Koran: A Very Short Introduction, pp. 30-33

The Epoch, sura 103. *Approaching the Koran*, p. 116 for interpretation, explanation p. 117

The Slander, sura 104. *Approaching the Koran*, p. 118 for interpretation, explanation p. 119

Sincerity/Unity, sura 112. *Approaching the Koran*, p. 136 for interpretation, explanation p. 137

Daybreak, sura 113. *Approaching the Koran*, p. 138 for interpretation, explanation p. 139

LECTURE FOUR: MOHAMMED

The Life of Mohammed, p. 117 (166, T.1171) trans. Guillaume

Gospel of John at 16:7-15

A Reader on Classical Islam, p. 45

A Reader on Classical Islam, p. 44

A Classical Reader on Islam, p. 11 for Adam; pp. 14-15 for Abraham

A Reader on Classical Islam, p. 54

Qur'an 2.260; Qur'an 3:19

A Reader on Classical Islam, p. 65 and p. 168

Qur'an 2.260; Qur'an 3.198

LECTURE FIVE: A HISTORY OF ISLAM: 570 TO 1600

Islam: A Short History, pp. 24-25

www.youtube.comTiny Toons Istanbul

www.youtube.com Afghan Shiites mark the day of Ashura

LECTURE SIX: A HISTORY OF ISLAM: 1600 TO 2011

www.youtube.com Mehter Marsi

Islam and the West, p. 19

www.youtube.com Orientalist Paintings, Middle East—HD

Islam: A Short History, pp. 148-149.

www.youtube.comThe Assassination of Anwar El Sadat

Islam and the West, pp. 139-140

Islam and the West, p. 39

Islam: A Short History, p. 189

Islam and the West, p. 41

www.sourcewatch.org.

www.youtube.com Saudi Arabia-Under the Veil

A Reader on Classical Islam, pp. 392-39

LECTURE SEVEN: PHILOSOPHY, SCIENCE, AND TECHNOLOGY

www.youtube.com Al Jazari- Master Engineer and Father of Robotics

Islam: A Short History, pp. 63-64, and for more detailed version, *A Reader on Classical Islam*, pp. 360-361

Islam: A Short History, p. 101

www.youtube.com Rumi Poem, Iranian Music and Divine Dance)

www.youtube.com Sayyid Qutb (9 minute 32 second excerpt from BBC documentary "the Power of Nightmares")

LECTURE EIGHT: LAW AND JURISPRUDENCE

Qur'an 45:18.

Story of Dinah, Genesis 34:1-34:31

www.youtube.com Capital Punishment: Shari'ah vs. Secular Law

A Reader on Classical Islam pp. 240-242; pp. 242-243

www.youtube.com The Sharia law –amputation in Nigeria; www.youtube.com Five women buried alive.

Islam and the West, pp. 52-3

Qur'an 2:275-2:276

In progression, Qur'an 2:219, 4:43, and 5:90

Qur'an 4:48

www.youtube.com Sadie BellyDance

1. *Islam: A Short History*, p. 16. 2. Lewis and Churchill, *Islam: The Religion and the People*, pp. 111-112. 3. Michael Cook, *The Koran: A Very Short Introduction*, p. 37

Selected passages from John L. Esposito, *Women in Muslim Family Law*, pp. 14-34.) Qur'an— Marriage: 24:32; Divorce: 2:226, 2:228, 2:229, 2:230, 2231; 2:240; 2:241; Widowhood: 2:233, 2:234

LECTURE NINE: PRAYER AND PREACHING

Call to prayer, CD track 1, *Approaching the Koran*. Explanation p. 150

www.youtube.com Mosques of the World—Islamic Architecture

A Classical Reader on Islam, p. 274

Qur'an 20:11-12

A Reader on Classical Islam, p. 12

The *Fatiha* (The Opening), CD track 2 from *Approaching the Koran*. 1. Explanation p. 156; or, www.youtube.com the best Fatiha soub. 2. *The Koran: A Very Short Introduction*, pp. 8-10

The Koran: A Very Short Introduction, pp. 77-79

Qur'an 2:30- 2:36

www.youtube.com How to Offer Prayers/Salat

www.youtube.com Rumi-Turning Esctatic: Scene

VOCABULARY: FEATURED WORDS AND TERMS

(Note: Given that there is no standard way to transliterate Arabic into English, alternate spellings of the following words and terms are possible.)

Abassid—second dynasty of Islamic rulers who were descendents of Mohammed's paternal uncle, Al-Abbas

Adat/Urf—local custom

Ahdan—the call to prayer

Ahl al kitab—People of the Book: Christians, Jews, and Muslims

Allah—literally, "the God"; the name of the Supreme Being in Islam

Al Qa'ida—literally "the base," but the name of the Islamic network led by Osama bin Laden

Al-sama' al-ula—body and soul

Amir—the commander, governor, chief of police, or head of army

Ansar—helper, specifically, the Medinans who first joined with Mohammed

'Aql—intellect, reason

'Asabiyyah—social cohesiveness

Ashab—companion, specifically, those who left Mecca with Mohammed

Ash'arite—An anti-rationalist school of philosophy and theology in the medieval period

Ayat—verse, especially in the Qur'an

Ayatollah—literally "faith," but by extension "religious leader"

Bayt al Hikma—House of Wisdom founded by Caliph Ma'mun

Bid'at—innovation, primarily in terms of Islamic religious practice or law

Bin/Bint—son of/daughter of (also "ibn"—son of)

Bismillah—the prayer invocation, "In the name of Allah, Most Gracious, Most Merciful"

Burqa—a long, loose-fitting garment with eye holes that completely covers a woman

Caliph/Khalifah—a successor to Mohammed, leader of the faithful. Also, khalifat Allah—Allah's caliph implying that the ruler is legitmate and upstanding; the "deputy" of Allah on Earth

Creatio ex nihilo—creation out of nothing which is the Christian vision of the origin of the world

Dar al Harb—the Zone of War; areas beyond Islamic lands

Dar al Islam—the House of Islam; all the Islamic lands

Darwesh—in Persian the word means "poor," but it is applied to Muslim mystics

Dhimmi/zhimmi—a community within an Islamic state that is not Islamic, but is protected by the state

Diaif—unreliable, especially as pertains to *hadith*

Entrepôt —a city that is dependent on facilitating trade on a trade route between other cities

Fakir—Muslim mystic

Falsafah—philosophy

Fiqh—law, religious law

Fasiq—impious, but redeemable by repentance; a transgressor

Fatiha—"The Opening" prayer; the first seven verses of the Qur'an

Faylasuf—philosopher

Fitnah—seduction; disorder. The word is used to designate the first Muslim civil war—a war that was to determine who was going to lead the faithful

Ghazi/Maghazi—raiding party(ies). The raiding tradition is Arabic tribal, and the idea carried over into the expansion of Islam for many centuries

Hadith—the narration of the teachings and actions of Mohammed, which are thought to be divinely inspired but are not in the Qur'an

Hajj—pilgrimage, especially the pilgrimage to Mecca as required by one of the Five Pillars

Hajji—one who has made the required pilgrimage to Mecca

Halal—permitted, legitimate, good, and often used in regard to Islamic food laws

Haram—forbidden

Hijira—migration, or the breaking of old ties; Mohammed's leaving Mecca for Medina in 622

Hikmah—wisdom

Hubal—vapor; spirit; also, the chief deity in the pre-Islamic Arabia; one of the many gods in *Jahiliya* before Mohammed's monotheism

Huddad—severe punishment based on a literal reading of the Qu'ran and hadith

Hukh—court judgment

Ibadat—ritual law and prayer; the believer's relationship to Allah

Ijma—consensus, especially group consensus as a way of interpreting some Islamic principle

Ijtihad—interpretation and reinterpretation of Islamic norms by Islamic scholars

Ikhwan al-Muslimun—Muslim Brotherhood, founded in Egypt in 1928

Ilhan—illumination, as in "divine illumination"

Ilm—knowledge, especially religious knowledge

Imam—literally means "in front of," but to Sh'ites it means "religious leader." It could also mean "(religious) belief" as in "keeping the faith"

Inshallah—"If Allah wills"; "Allah willing." A phrase used frequently after a statement of desire

Islam—literally this means "submission," by implication "submission to the will of God"

Islamicist—a scholar who studies the Islamic faith and culture

Islamist—a strong advocate for the Islamic faith and culture

Isnad—the line of repeaters of the *hadith* of Mohammed from Mohammed to his companions to his followers

Jahiliya—confusion; the period before the birth of Mohammed; a godless non-Islamic world

Jama'ah—the mosque's congregation

Jihad—to struggle; popularly interpreted as "holy war"

Jinn—spoken of in the Quran at sura 72, they are spirits of the earth created by fire. They can bring both fortune and misfortune

Jizra—poll tax

Kaaba—the sacred temple in Mecca

Kafir—unbeliever, often used with emotion as a derogatory slur

Kalam—logic; Arab scholasticism

Madhab—school of jurisprudence

Madrassa—an Islamic school primarily for teaching the religion

Mahdi—a final eschatological redeemer and ultimate religious and political guide

Mecca—the city of Mohammed's birth, the location of the Kaaba, and site of the hajj

Medina—originally called Yatrib, the city Mohammed goes to after leaving Mecca. "Medina" also means "city," and "din" means "Law," so medina might be "the law-governed place" and therefore different from the countryside.

Mihnah—inquisition; religiously motivated inquisition

Mihrab—niche in a wall of a mosque indicating the direction of Mecca

Minbar—pulpit

Mi'raj—Mohammed's "night journey" from Mecca to the highest heaven.

Mosque—literally this means "a place to prostrate oneself; a house of worship

Mu'amalat—deeds, contracts; moral relations between people

Muezzin—the one who calls the faithful to prayer

Mufti—one qualified to render legal opinions

Mujtahid—the religious scholars and teachers. In Iran the mujtahid have great political authority

Mullah—leader of prayer at a mosque; a teacher of the Qur'an

Muslim—true believer (pronounced, "moose leem")

Mutakallimum—roughly, theologians, generally of a conservative perspective

Mu'tazilites—seceders, schismatics, "those who keep themselves apart." An early philosophical and theological school of thought, which was both rationalist and humanistic

Nasik—abrogation, especially of a former Qur'anic principle

Nikah—marriage contract, or by popular implication, simply, marriage

Orientalist—a term originating in the nineteenth century used to classify Western scholars who studied Arab cultures

Qadi—the judge in a court of law

Qiblah—facing toward Mecca

Qiyas—analogy; legal scholars may "extend by analogy" principles laid out in the Qur'an

Qur'an/Koran—the recitations of Mohammed of Allah's words which were fashioned into the Islamic sacred text

Rak'ah—a sequence of prayer and gesture

Rashidun—the first four caliphs, all of whom are considered orthodox

Regnum and sacerdotum—royalty and church implying a division between the secular sphere of life and the religious sphere

Riddah—apostasy, especially "the wars of Riddah" in 632

Sahih—reliable, sound, especially hadith

Salafiist—a Muslim who advocates a return to the first years of the faith, the period of the Rashidun

Salam—peace

Salat—worship, prayer

Sawm—fasting

Shahada—the Islamic creed; the first of the Five Pillars of the Islamic faith

Shari'a—holy law; the ideal law founded on the Qur'an

Shatan—Satan, the devil

Shayk—leader, distinguished old man

Shi'a—the branch of Islam that claims descent from Ali

Shirk—an act of serious unrighteousness

Shura—consultation, as in a body of Muslim advisers who confer and give advice to a caliph or sultan

Suf—a woolen cloak; the word along with *faqir* and *darwesh*, meaning "poor," becomes the name of Muslim mystics, "Sufi"

Sufi—Muslim mystic

Sultan—political leader

Sunna—the actual teachings and actions of Mohammed as told in *hadith* (some scholars do not distinguish between *sunna* and *hadith*)

Sunni—the largest branch of Islam; Muslims who claim to be following the *sunna*

Sura—a chapter of the Qur'an

Tabish—prayer beads, rosary

Tafsir—exegesis; learned commentary on the Qur'an

Tahil—the phrase "no god but Allah" in the opening of the Islamic creed

Takbir—the phrase "Allah is the Greatest"

Taliban—Truth-seekers; students from *madrasas* who controlled Afghanistan in 1990s

Taqiyya—dissimulation

Taqlid—following a tradition, especially a specific tradition advocated by a madhab

Tariqa—a Sufi order, brotherhood

Tasawwuf—Islamic mysticism

Tawhid—oneness; the singularity of Allah

Ulama/ulema—a group of religious scholars

Umayyad—first dynasty of Islamic rulers

Umma—the community of believers

Wahabism—a conservative branch of Islam which follows the teachings of Ibn abd al Wahab (d.1792) centered in Saudi Arabia

Waqf—a pious foundation for helping the poor, widows, and orphans

Wazir—a government high official; an adviser

Za'iraja—astrology

Zakat—lierally "purity"; a tax; monies given as charity

Zikr/ dhikr—Sufi meditation techniques; mystical activities as in the repeated "recollection" of the name of Allah

FOR FURTHER DISCUSSION

TECHNOLOGY AND INVENTIONS OF ISLAM'S CLASSICAL PERIOD

Philosophy, science, and technology were first promoted in *Dar al Islam* when Caliph Ma'mun in the early ninth century founded the *Bayt al Hikma* in Baghdad. The *Bayt al Hikma* was an institution of higher learning where scholars studied Greco-Roman, Persian, Indian, and Egyptian source material, and ideas found in earlier philosophical and scientific writings were developed under Qur'anic influence. In the applied sciences, technological innovations occurred in medicine; alchemy; agronomy; and astronomy, astrology, and other math-based studies.

There has been much discussion among scholars as to how Greco-Roman philosophy, science, and technology were transferred to the Arabs and then other Muslim ethnicities. One suggestion is that such material came into Arab and Persian hands when in 529 the Byzantine Emperor Justinian closed the schools of philosophy throughout the Byzantine Empire. Justinian did not like the philosophers who had rejected Christianity, and so when their school were closed they fled with their precious libraries eastward beyond the borders of Justinian's empire into Arab and Persian lands. Given such material and later accruals of manuscripts from India, Egypt, and Persia, such a wealth of material could only inspire further developments.

Though the Bayt al Hikma was the first, it was followed by "schools" at Isfahan, Toledo, Cairo (the still open Al Ahzar University), and Palermo. Much was done with source material by Islamic scholars heralding from a wide variety of heritages beyond Arabia during the first five or six centuries of Islam. Here is a sampling of some of the more important Muslim discoveries and technological innovations.

Eighth century:

- Baghdad streets are paved with tar.

- Ibn Hayyan invents numerous laboratory devices to further his work in alchemy. He improves techniques for distillation, crystallization, filtration, and liquefaction.

Ninth century:

- A workable, vertical axle windmill appears in Persia.

- <u>Al-Khwarizmi</u> publishes *The Compendious Book on Calculation by Completion and Balancing*. The book is the foundational statement for *al-jabr (algebra)*.

- The Musa brothers publish the *Book of Ingenious Devices*. Their devices include such musical instruments as a water powered organ and a mechanical flute player. They also list a trick drinking vessel and a hurricane lamp.

Tenth century:

- Engineers invent a variety of surveying instruments.

- Ibn Zakariya Razi (Rhazes) describes the chemical processes of amalgamation, calcination, and sublimation.

- Kerosene is produced from the distillation of petroleum.

Eleventh century:

- Ammar ibn Ali publishes the *Choice of Eye Diseases*. He is also the inventor the hollow metal syringe hypodermic needle.

- Glass mirrors are being manufactured in southern Spain.

- Al Zahrawi publishes the thirty-volume medical encyclopedia, the *Al Tasrif*, which is the standard medical text in Muslim and European universities until the sixteenth century. He also invents the plaster cast, cotton dressing, and various forms of anesthesia.

- The purification process for potassium nitrate was first described in *Al-Muqaddimat* by Ibn Bakhtawayh.

- Al Biruni was the first to apply the experimental method to mechanics, especially the fields of statics and dynamics. He claimed that light has a finite speed and said that light's speed is much faster than that of sound.. He said that the Earth rotated on its axis. He invented the mechanical astrolabe, employing with eight gear functions.

Twelfth century:

- Al Khazini publishes *The Book of the Balance of Wisdom*. He describes a variety of scientific instruments including the steelyard balance and hydrostatic balance. He also brings the experimental method to statics and dynamics.

Thirteenth century:

- Al Jazari publishes *The Book of Knowledge of Ingenious Mechanical Devices*. In well-drawn pictures he describes a variety of devices including mechanical clocks and gear-regulated robots.

- Gun powder and simple hand-held cannons are developed by Egyptian craftsmen.

- Ibn Khaldun publishes the *Muqaddimah*. A social science treatise, it presents a variety of concepts, including social conflict, networking, and economic growth.

Islamic education for scholars-to-be was not a matter of going to a university and taking a series of classes and then getting a diploma. Future scholars traveled about from city to city and from master to master, gaining what knowledge they could. Information was frequently transmitted orally, and memorization (often of entire books) was a central part of the educational process. Scholars were well versed not in just one field but several, though often either the field of *fiqh* (law) or medicine was the primary one. Other fields of study included astronomy, mathematics, music, logic, and philosophy.

Over the centuries *Dar al Islam* produced a great array of *faylasuf* (philosophers), scientists, and social commentators. Good work was done in astronomy, medicine, chemistry, and metaphysics during these centuries, and numerous histories of science texts and essays have reviewed and saluted this success.

And now—What would you say?

FOR FURTHER DISCUSSION

THE DECLINE OF PHILOSOPHY AND SCIENCE IN DAR AL ISLAM AFTER THE 13ᵀᴴ CENTURY

Muslim philosophers viewed *falsafah* as a study which transforms the mind and the soul and which is never separated from the spiritual purity and ultimate sanctity that *hikmah* connotes in Islamic culture. Moreover, some Muslim scholars said that *ilm* was limited only to what could be known for certain and that would be God and the Qur'an.

Until modern times philosophy and science were not really distinct. Philosophy was simply divided between moral philosophy (metaphysics generally) and natural philosophy (a grand, universal scheme uniting all of nature). So it is fair to treat Muslim philosophy and science as a single discipline.

Interesting Case of Decline

Ibn Nadim, author of *Kitab al Fihrist*, (a tenth century index of Arab literature), reported that in the ninth century 1,416 secular works were produced in Islamic lands. However, by the fourteenth century the number had dropped to 305. Nevertheless, it wasn't only the number of scholarly writings that decreased; what was produced was of inferior intellectual quality. Astrology was considered a science, and an important one, in *Dar al Islam*, but by the twelfth century the astronomical observations that served astrology had been degraded into worthless mystical tables and charts. Why did decline set in?

The Power of Faith

When causes for the decline of science and philosophy in *Dar al Islam* are cited, usually the first named is the faith itself. There is a good reason for this, for Islamic theology leaves no room for a purely secular realm. The Muslim world is a sacred world, one without the mundane or profane, where every action and every event carries the idea of an all-pervading Islamic world. If a culture becomes totally permeated by its religion, so that no secular or "profane" realm exists, science will have an impossible task trying to survive. In a culture where the religion and members of the religious authority have fashioned the entirety of reality, there is no possibility of independent thinking in the sciences and philosophy.

Another "argument from faith" is based on a theory of personal motivation. The argument claims that faith acts to stifle independent scholarly work, if the scholar lives in a faith-culture that deprecates such work, and the scholar himself worries that his culture might be right in that assessment. In other words, there would be a sense of self-doubt or even stronger, shame, about what one is doing, because what one is doing is ultimately felt to be wrong by the doer, and all that is needed to be pushed "over the edge" is the warnings of the enforcers of the dominant perspective. Hence, the third "argument from faith" is offered, which answers the issue of specificity.

Nevertheless, though there is much to recommend both of these arguments, they lack the specificity that would remove them from the realm of sociological and psychological generalities. Hence, the following, third "argument from faith," which answers the issue of specificity, is presented.

Caliph Ma'mun (c. 820) had a dream in which Aristotle appeared and told him to study the works of the Greek philosophers. In 833 he founded the *Bayt al Hikma* (House of Wisdom), an institution of higher learning, and there scholars lived by the principle that religious texts should accord with reason—their own and the Greeks'.

Ma'mun found support for his ideas in a group of rationalist theologians, the Mu'tazilites (roughly, "those who keep themselves apart"). The Mu'tazilites maintained that Allah had given people a free will and that the Qur'an was created by Allah, and as a creation, it was not quite as sacrosanct as Allah. From this it followed for the Mu'tazilites that scholars could freely subject the Qur'an to rational study and the tools of Greek logic. However, the conservative Ash'arites (disciples of Abu 'l-Hasan al Ash'ari—interestingly, as a young man he was a Mu'tazilite) and prominent scholars such as Ahmad ibn Hanbal (780-855) maintained that people were under the constant, unwavering direction of Allah and the Qur'an was Allah's eternal word, co-eternal with Allah and a part of Allah, and as such must be beyond the prying of rational analysis and interpretation. After much squabbling and what could be considered religious inquisitions, theologians who advocated divine determinism and the uncreatedness of the Qur'an carried the day. Mu'tazilitism was banished, the *Bayt al Hikma* faded into history, and rationalism suffered an enormous defeat, the magnitude of which would grow larger as centuries passed.

As Islam developed, not only the Mu'tazalites, but others were offering interpretations ("*ijithad*," which also means "independent thinking") of the Qur'an. By the tenth century the majority of Muslim scholars held that there had been too much interpretation, and so they insisted that only the great scholars of the past had the right to *ijithad*. When the door to *ijithad* was finally closed (the famous eleventh century theologian al Ghazzali and his book *Tahafut al-falasifa*, *The Incoherence of the Philosophers*, played a central role in this), the spirit of inquiry suffered a terrible blow and soon the demand of *taqlid* (blind following) arose, which fit nicely with determinism. Islam became a religion with no avenue for independent thinking—a religion that could only look backward and sustain a culture that gloried in the past.

The Power of Mysticism and the Supernatural

There is a wide vein of mysticism running through Islam, and that, too, had a dampening effect on science and philosophy. Mystical intuitionism coupled with an extreme rationalism's complete rejection of close empirical observation can only lead to the demise of science and philosophy. Of course, the mysticism that permeates Islam came not only from the Qur'an, its earliest interpreters, or al Ghazzali, but also from the former beliefs of the many people that came under the sway of the religion. What is important is that the Muslim mystical landscape of Islam could easily lead to a lack of interest in science and blindness to the discoveries of Europe's seventeenth century "mechanical philosophy."

But we cannot leave mysticism just yet. Astrology is one form that mysticism can take, and astrology was endemic in the cultures through which Islam spread. There is no evidence that Islamic jurists and other scholars attempted to suppress astrology (as was the case in Europe); in fact, the Sufis embraced it. Of interest here is that astrology requires a small and geocentric universe, if any sense is to be made of the practice. The universe must have an equatorial band crossing the band of the zodiac, and the twelve groupings of stars, the zodiac constellations, must be actual groupings, not stars innumerable light years apart. Moreover, the Earth and its inhabitants must be special, not just one of a myriad of inhabited planets, and be in the center of the cosmos. Hence, the Copernican Revolution, though it faced enormous challenges in the West, would have faced even greater ones in the East.

And the Copernican Revolution was part and parcel of the Scientific Revolution and the new "mechanical philosophy" of Newton and others. Europe's "mechanical philosophy" depended upon the belief that cause and effect relations exist between certain states of affairs. Cause and effect is the binder, the glue that forever holds the cosmos together. As Newton and other seventeenth century and Enlightenment scientists came to believe, not even God could break this bond, and the thought that God would order a miracle came to be seen as defamation of the divinity's character, because it implied that God had made a mistake and a miracle was required to fix it.

But such was not the case in Islamic conceptions of the universe. That Allah determined all that happened meant that the relations between various states of affairs, each and every one, were ordained by Allah, each and every time, at the whim of Allah who was certainly not constrained by any mere mechanical laws. It was the eleventh century theologian Al Ghazzali who maintained that Allah exercised His infinite prerogatives at will and constantly intervened in the world. Taken to its logical extreme, this meant that no event was of necessity conjoined with another. Much of this idea remains alive today in a Muslim's personal behavior as every sentence that speaks to a future occurrence is followed by the phrase "Allah willing."

The Destruction from War

Historians of Islamic culture often point to the reoccurring destruction caused by war in *Dar al Islam*. Hence, one needs to observe that here, too, is a contributor to the decline and elimination of science and philosophy.

Often, though not always, Islam was spread by the sword. There was large-scale warfare and there were small raids (*maghazi*). There are instances when a declined invitation to become Muslim was viewed as a reason to forcibly convert a neighboring non-Islamic state. Then again, one Islamic state might attack another Islamic state with the justification that the latter was not Islamic enough or Islamic in the right way. Such warfare was constant enough to insure an instability in which science and philosophy would have difficulty flourishing.

Far and away the most significant instance of instability caused by warfare was the Mongol invasions, beginning with Genghis Khan's in the thirteenth century and ending with Timur's (Tamerlane) in the late fourteenth century. The Mongols spread absolute havoc and brought ruin wherever they went. And it is this destruction some historians cite as the single most important cause for the end of Islamic science and philosophy.

The breakdown of Islamic civilization was undoubtedly accelerated by the arrival of new waves of barbarians from the steppe lands. The Turks and Mongols by themselves, however, would never have been able to overrun the Islamic lands and effectively sterilize their culture by the thirteenth century, had these been in a flourishing economic state. That invasion alone is not a sufficient explanation is shown by the contemporary decline in Egypt and North Africa, into which the Mongols never penetrated.

The Education Establishment

Certainly, the roots of the concept of institutionalized higher learning existed in the early centuries of Islam for we find communities of scholars at work in such centers of learning as Toledo, Cordoba, Palermo, Bukhara, Samarkand, and Baghdad. Yet the idea of a university where institutionalized learning and a strict program of study was carried on failed to develop. One possible cause for why the university system or research society failed to develop may have been the lack of government support. Nor is there anything resembling the "Royal science societies" or publication networks that developed in the West.

What did transpire in Islamic states was a system of education based on the personal transmission of information. A student would study with a particular scholar, and that scholar after a suitable period of time and approving of what the student learned authorized that student to teach in the scholar's name. After a student had satisfied a particular scholar, the student would then travel, often great distances, to another scholar, to glean other insights and more information.

Whatever the cause, in Islamic states science remained a craft, and insights were passed down in scholar-disciple, master-apprentice, or father-son relations. For example, medical knowledge was passed from master to apprentice in hospitals, rather than in college and graduate school biology, anatomy, and physiology classes, and teaching hospitals. Moreover, scientific and philosophic research was valued for the "applied" technology it provided in medicine, agriculture, mechanical engineering, and warfare, not for the abstract pursuits of "pure science."

Given the lack of a formalized educational apparatus for advanced studies in science and philosophy, and the conception that only religious studies produce knowledge, the former were bound to deteriorate. Here, therefore, is one more factor necessary to include when determining what happened to science and philosophy in Islamic states.

"Islamic Science"

Interestingly, the idea that there is something called "Islamic science" was operative almost from the birth of Islam and is still operative today in the minds of many Muslims who bemoan the fact that *Dar al Islam* has fallen so far behind the West. But it is the very notion that there could and should be something called "Islamic science" that prevents objective philosophic speculation and eliminates scientific research in Islamic cultures.

What Islam failed to realize is that there is no such thing as Islamic science, because science is not Islamic, Christian, or anything else. Of course, scientists and philosophers have a cultural, or ethnic, or religious identity, and science may be done in Christian, Muslim, or Hindu lands, but the discoveries of science and philosophy are not Christian or whatever in themselves. And those who want science done in a fashion that somehow conforms to or deductively derives from sacred scripture or political manifesto, won't do any science.

Again and again one finds books and journals that begin with a prayer to Allah before reviewing the condition of scientific research and philosophical analysis in *Dar al Islam*. Science is not religion, and a culture that has no secular sphere will have no science or philosophy. Moreover, Islamic metaphysics does not distinguish between facts about nature and Islamic moral values: Where everything possesses an Islamic moral value, a neutral, secular science of fact, hypothesis, and theory cannot survive.

Conclusion

No single event can account for the decline and elimination of science and philosophy in *Dar al Islam*. Some causes may be more important than others, but it is a confluence of several causes that brought about the decline sometime in the High Middle Ages and the elimination by the fifteenth century. Significant causes include the role of a powerful theology coupled with an all-powerful *ulama*, mysticism, war, education, and a misunderstanding regarding the independence of science and philosophy. And, as has been shown, some things that writers have cited as causes are too general, or cannot be accurately assessed as to their effects, or are simply wrong.

And now—What would you say?

FOR FURTHER DISCUSSION

MARTYRDOM AND TERRORISM

Fundamental ethical principles are embedded in the Qur'an, the Christian Bible, and the Jewish Tenakh. These profound structural determinants are just that, because they do not frame one piece of behavior, but rather an entire social outlook, an existential ordering of personal life and social interaction. For example, what a religion's sacred scripture contends about the value of one's own life and the life of others determines how one leads his or her life and conceives the greater social reality.

These three revelations are offered to humankind as a direct word from God, and each of the faiths based on these books claims the status of Ultimate and Final Truth. However, even a cursory review of these three faiths finds renderings of the Ultimate and Final Truth that are often far from identical, similar, or even harmonious. If, therefore, philosophers or theologians were to make a claim for a universal ethics, an immutable and eternal set of Truths founded on a revelation from God, they would have to perform some serious intellectual juggling. If philosophers and theologians address but one issue, the value of human life, they are confronted by the mystery that God found it necessary to reveal three different scriptures, at least with the appearance of three different ethical determinants dealing with the taking of human life.

Universality might be saved by saying that the revelations are the same; it is just that the human interpretations of them differ. There is something to that suggestion, no doubt, but not enough. Yes, these ethical principles are filtered through interpretive judgments by Christian theologians, rabbis and Beth Din, Catholic Canon Law experts, and the ulama and Qur'anic scholars, yet these principles still remain as structural determinants of a wide variety of behaviors.

What is operative here is that two layers of ethical concern exist: an absolutely fundamental, revelation-seated principle and then, a second layer, an interpretative construction on the first layer. Yet the point is not that we move from the universal and abstract principle to a practical application—a Natural Law sort of approach that all too frequently has ended in tortured casuistry. Rather the point is that the fundamental principle, via the interpretive process, will be mollified or made draconian. In other words, the interpretive process is not a matter of saying that x is a universal principle that should be applied here but not there, or this is how x should be applied to situation y. Rather by mollification a law that says x will become x-, while by severity it will become x+. Hence, we are not going from a universal ethical determinant to a particular moral situation, but from a framework–making maxim, a parameter defining determinant, to a quality-adjusting interpretative judgment. The ethical determinant controls the direction any modifications will take and limits what can be considered a modification and what can be ruled out as a complete debasement.

In a discussion of the value of human life, people are confronted by the perplexity that God found it necessary to reveal three different ethical principles dealing with the self-appropriation of one's time of death in the service of a larger cause. The issue here is martyrdom: utilizing the termination of one's own life as a visible dedication to a belief or a cause. This is different from suicide, which is ending one's life because of something amiss in that life.

The histories of Islam, Christianity, and Judaism provide many examples of what has been read as martyrdom.

Jewish scriptures relate the story of Samson and Delilah, the death of Saul, and Jewish history revels in the battle at Masada. When Samson pulls the pillars of the hall down on himself, we have a case of someone taking his own life and all those gathered about. In regard to Saul, we read at Samuel 31:4:

> The Philistines hotly pursued Saul and . . . killed his three sons . . . . [And] some archers came upon him [Saul] and he was wounded . . . . So he said to his armour-bearer, "Draw your sword and run me through, so that these uncircumcised brutes may not come . . . and make sport of me." But the armour-beater refused . . . . whereupon Saul took his own sword and fell on it.

Finally, in the story of Masada, the besieged Jews die by their own hand rather than surrender to the Romans.

From the early years of Christianity comes the story of Vibia Perpetua joyously looking forward to her martyrdom in the Roman arena. She was about to prove the power of her faith to Christians who were imprisoned with her and to the pagans who had come to watch the show. She was a young woman, and she carried a baby in her arms.

From the Islamic faith we find the recent event of a young women who had decided to strap explosives to her body and blow herself up on a crowded Israeli street. This young woman was going to prove the power of her faith in Islam and her belief in the Palestinian cause by giving her life and taking with her many Israelis. She was in her late twenties and had a seven-year-old child.

In reviewing these scenarios, we are faced with two distinct sets of issues. First, to what ethical determinants can each of these individuals who have taken their life appeal in their own faith tradition? Second, what do these three scenarios tell us about the act of martyrdom?

First: Looking at these scenarios, it is not obvious that each can be justified by ethical determinants in the revelatory deliverances of scriptures claimed to be directly and infallibly delivered by God or His angelic messengers.

The Islamic faith clearly does sanction martyrdom, going so far in *suras* 4:66 and 4:69 as to promote it as a true test of faith. Martyrs are part of the Fourfold Fellowship of Faith: Prophets who Teach; Sincere Believers of the Truth; Witnesses who Testify (martyrs); and the Righteous who do Good. Whatever meaning scholars wish to give to "Jihad," whether it is simply "to struggle" or by extension to struggle in defense of the faith, or "Holy War," sure access to heaven is to die in defending the faith.

Christianity in its formative years gained the title "Church of the Martyrs," and many Christian martyrs the Catholic Church recognizes as saints. Vibia Perpetua, St. Perpetua, was only one of many. But it is unclear if Christian scripture provides an ethical determinant, a direct pronouncement that one is to sacrifice himself or herself. Paul speaks of winning a victory wreath for keeping the faith no matter what may come, and early iconography depicts a laurel crown for athletes for Christ. Yet, nowhere is martyrdom for the faith specifically ordered.

As for Judaism, the case is clear: Judaism does not sanction martyrdom, in spite of the occurrence of Jewish martyrs. The commandment, "Thou shall not murder," applies both to others and oneself. And as the Qur'an points out, "Thou will find them [Jews], Of all people, most greedy/Of life" (2:96).

Now, to the second set of issues. By analyzing each of these scenarios we can see that what occurs is far from a straightforward case of martyrdom. Initially, we must decide whether we are viewing a suicide, martyrdom, or execution, or some blend of these. In order to decide this, we must ask the following questions: "What else could this person have done?" "Could he/she have lived on?" "When death is absolutely immanent, is it better to die by one's own hand or by another's?" These and similar questions make one hesitate before identifying the action as martyrdom.

Second, we must decide if an individual's choice for martyrdom becomes a choice enforced on others. Here we observe that love of a personal belief, ideology, or dogma may rank higher than respect for other people or love of family or offspring. (That dying for a cause ranks higher than love of one's own life is a given here.) In some cases martyrs take, either directly or indirectly, others with them to death. The death of a mother may bring with it the death or at least the destruction of a child. Suicide bombers take with them as many as they are able. We are forced to consider whether one has the right to make a decision for others who may or may not hold similar or any ideological views. Furthermore, we must decide if the people who were killed by the bomber should be considered martyrs, too. If we make a decision for others and they are thought of as martyrs, can one, therefore, become a martyr without freely willing it?

Third, we must ask when does a martyr for the faith become a martyr because of, or to the faith? Here, we observe that it is altogether possible that a particular ethical determinant is given a draconian interpretation by a priesthood, prophet, or ruling clergy, and the adherent may find himself both dedicated to his religion and victimized by the interpretation of its ethical principles. In other words, the demands put on the parishioner may make of him not a martyr for his faith but a martyr to his faith. Someone may end up with his highest aspiration's being the desire to prove that he is a faithful adherent to a creed, rather than living as a moral individual as defined by the creed's ethical determinants.

Can we draw any conclusions from all these considerations? First, we can say that not everything that gets called martyrdom is such—distinctions must be made. Second, if a martyr destroys the lives of others, those who die along with the martyr were not treated as agents but as objects. Making decisions for others fails to treat them as subjects in their own right, especially if we use them to further our own ends without consideration of their choices. Third, martyrdom may pit the individual against a priesthood demanding loyalty not to a set of ethical determinants but a draconian evaluation of those determinants expressed in a religion's orthodoxy or orthopraxy. And lastly, if these three revelations, Qur'an, Bible, and Tanakh, have a divine origin, then either God is confused or for some unfathomable reason He wishes to confuse us. The World so wants to believe that no matter what name is given to the Supreme Being, people are all following the lead of the same one, and no one wants to believe that either an omniscient god is divinely confused or takes pleasure in baffling his human creations.

And now—What would you say?

FOR FURTHER DISCUSSION

DEMOCRACY AND THE NATION-STATE

There has been much discussion regarding the possibility of bringing democracy to Muslim states. One argument has it that democratic institutions will counter tribalism, suppression of the poor, revenge-based practices, and social and gender inequality. No matter the real or supposed virtues of democracy, the first question would be, just what is a democratic state? Of course, the second question, less theoretical but certainly more important, is do Muslims, whether political leaders, intellectuals, or the common folk, want a democracy?

As to the first question, what constitutes a democratic system, the following list probably would suffice.

1. Open to all comers, meaning at least two political parties, implying pluralism in place of authoritarianism or totalitarianism

2. Unhampered electoral process, meaning a secure ballot box and freedom from intimidation or retribution

3. An independent judiciary with enforceable sanctions—a division of governmental powers

4. A free, non-censorable, non-coercible press

5. Issues-based politics and programs in a search for a common ground and common good, rather than ideology-driven programs or tribal or ethnic allegiance-politics

6. Promulgated universal law (equality before the law) and guaranteed universal rights

7. The state as prosecutor in place of personal revenge

Of course, such practices are not easy to develop, especially when people have not had a tradition of personal independence nor a desire for it. Democratic ideas and institutions based on trusting the "common folk" and seeing the government as responsible to the people rather than the people being servants of the government took a long time to develop in Western democracies. The first philosophical writings on the promises of democracy do not appear until the seventeenth century.

Moreover, maintaining a democracy is a very difficult thing to do. In times of trouble who does not look to a single strong leader, a messiah, savior, or *madhi*? The experience of the Great Depression (1929-1939) and its effects on Germany, Italy, and other nations is proof enough of this phenomenon.

One good way of understanding the difference between Muslim political philosophy and Western is to see Muslim political practices, *Shari'a*, and *fiqh* as rooted in a Middle Eastern tribal culture and Western political philosophy as European state-based practices. Western theory, founded on Roman republican ideals and Stoicism, suggests a state which places distance between individuals and allows for laws that are to be applied in a similar fashion to all citizens. In tribal law, relationships between people are left at a private, personal level as are relations between the individual and leadership. In fact, in tribal systems the idea of individuality, or rather, personhood, is far less acknowledged than the structures of family, clan, and tribe.

Given a tribal system of governance, actions from marriage to murder can be treated through inter- and intra-family rituals of contract, barter, and revenge. In Western law, though a judge has some discretion in settling sanctions, it is the state that prosecutes and determines the outcome, not the parties involved. Unlike in a *Shari'a* legal system, under Western jurisprudence one family cannot offer to another money to settle a murder.

Under tribal systems universally applicable laws can exist, but with the understanding that leadership is beyond the law and leaders can contravene the law. In tribal systems, the cry of the populace is for justice; individual liberty is not a pervasive interest because one is not an individual but a member of a family. Justice is what is important if decisions can be of any sort. With well-functioning democratic institutions, the cry of the populace is for liberty to do what as individuals they might wish to do. Justice has been secured by equal application of law.

For Westerners the best way to understand tribalism is to read the Hebrew Scriptures, particularly Genesis. The story of Dinah makes a fascinating excursion into tribalism with its principles of revenge and rule by patriarchy. By the time of the later Jewish-Hellenistic writings and the Christian New Testament, Roman law and jurisprudence had replaced tribalism, and the effect of this in late sacred writings is obvious.

As to the second question, whether Muslims want to live with democratic institutions, many Muslim scholars point out that the Qur'an has nothing to say regarding constitutional government and by extension the argument is made that democracy and constitutional government are un-Islamic. Election by the mass of people is not mentioned; rather, the notion of obedience and submission is the by-word of the holy book. The closest thing to popular sovereignty that is found in Muslim forms of government is the *shura*, a council of *shayks* who confer with and give advice to the tribal leader (something like an American president's cabinet), but the final decision is up to the tribal chieftain, sultan, or caliph.

Many scholars would contend that since the Qur'an is the word of Allah, then only a theocracy is the proper form of government. The Islamic Republic of Iran views itself as a theocratic republic, governed by *Shari'a* law and a unicameral *Majles e Shura ye Eslami* (Consultative Assembly). The modern Egyptian philosopher Sayyid Qutb wrote that democracy was a Western invention incompatible with the "divine sovereignty" enjoined by Islam. When in 1991 in Algeria the "first-round elections" were won by the fundamentalists, they claimed, "It's victory for Islam, not for democracy."

And now—What would you say?

FOR FURTHER DISCUSSION

DIFFERENCES BETWEEN SUNNI AND SHI'ITE ISLAM

Within a quarter century of Mohammed's death, Islam was embroiled in a civil war (656-661) that split the religion into two competing sects. The divide occurred because of a dispute over how the leadership of the Muslim community should be determined: many Muslims believed that a consensus of the *umma*'s leaders should decide the selection of a caliph, while others believed that the caliph should come from the family and descendants of Mohammed. The former group became known as the Sunnis, because they viewed themselves as followers of the actions (*sunna*) of Mohammed. The latter group, the Shi'ites (the party of Ali), saw themselves as followers of the cousin and son-in-law of Mohammed, Ali, and his descendants. Over the centuries, though both groups continued to share an almost identical Qur'an and a multitude of activities, fundamental differences in worship, philosophy, and daily practices arose.

As it happened, the first four caliphs were selected by consensus. Yet, despite the fact that the consensus criterion prevailed, many Muslims continued to argue that leadership should remain in Mohammed's family as there was something special about Mohammed and that exceptionality lay in the family "blood". Though the first four caliphs were chosen using the consensus criterion, the fourth, Ali, obviously met both criteria.

In 656 a civil war broke out when Muawiyyah ibn Ali Sufyan claimed the caliphate and rejected Ali's leadership. The details of the war and its lead up may never be clear, as the exact politics and actions of the period are given very different readings in the legends and stories of the time. What can be said with certainty is that Islam split in two: one faction would become known as the Shi'ites while a second would become known as the Sunnis. In Sunni history, Ali is the fourth caliph and Muawiyyah is the fifth; in Shi'ite history, Ali is the fourth caliph and first imam and Muawiyyah was a usurper.

Ali was assassinated in 661 by a member of a Muslim splinter sect, the Kharijites, who were unhappy that Ali appeared ready to appease and compromise with Muawiyyah. After Ali's death his second-born son, Hasan, became the imam, but he was assassinated six months into the imamnate. Husayn ibn Ali, Ali's third-born son then became the sect's imam. Meanwhile, Muawiyyah was intent on founding the Umayyad dynasty and when he died, his son, Yazid I (645 to 683), was proclaimed caliph. Husayn ibn Ali would not swear allegiance to Yazid, and at Karbala in 680, Husayn and his entire family and associates were killed Yazid's troops. This sealed the division between Sunni and Shi'ite, and to the present day great tension exists between Sunnis and Shi'ites.

At present, the Shi'ite sect constitutes approximately fifteen to twenty per cent of the billion and a half Muslim faithful. Iran is approximately ninety per cent Shi'ite, while Shi'ites are the majority in Iraq, Yemen, and Bahrain. The reason for the high numbers of Shi'ite in Iran and Iraq is found in the actions of Shah Ismail I (1487-1524), founder of the Safavid dynasty, who declared Shi'ite Islam the official religion of his empire. On the other hand, Saudi Arabia, Pakistan, Turkey, Jordan, and Egypt are overwhelmingly Sunni.

Though Sunnis and Shi'ites share the Qur'an along with a long list of *sunna* and *hadith* as their authoritative texts, there are fundamental differences between them as regards the leadership of the *umma*, the adoration of Ali and Husayn, the existence of later prophets, the correct understanding of the Qur'an and Shari'a, and the role of emotion in the religion. For example:

- Leadership. Significant differences exist in the structure and organization of the religious leadership between Shi'ites and Sunni. There is a Shi'ite clergy hierarchy, and religious and political authority is placed in the most learned spiritual leaders. No such hierarchy exists among the Sunnis.

- Ali and Husayn. Shi'ite Islam places great emphasis on the source of their sect. The Day of Ashurra is a day of commemoration of the deaths of Husayn and his family.

- Prophet-hood. Though for both Sunni and Shi'ite Mohammed is the greatest of prophets, for Sunnis he is the last of the prophets, while for Shi'ite there exist prophets after Mohammed. Shi'ites believe that a string of prophet-imams followed on Ali and Husayn, and that this prophet-hood did not come to an end until the twelfth imam, who did not die but rather hid himself away and one day will return as the *madhi*. By some accounts, the Ayatollah Ruhollah Khomeini, the leader of the 1979 Revolution in Iran almost succeeded in having himself declared the returned twelfth imam.

- Ethics: Martyrdom among Shi'ites is more extensively adhered to than among Sunni; many suicide bombers are of the Shi'ite faith and see their death as the ultimate jihad. A similar ethic was seen in the Iran-Iraq war as many Iranian youth fought in suicide brigades.

- Shari'a: Though both Sunni and Shi'ite scholars rely on the *sunna*, *hadith*, and Qur'an to develop sharia and fiqh, the Shia give preference to those *hadith* and *sunna* that are believed to have their source and proof in Mohammed's family and close friends. The Sunnis, on the other hand, say that the *hadith* and *sunna* of the twelve thousand "companions' of Mohammed are valid.

- Lawful practices. Certain legal principles are at variance between Shi'ite and Sunni. Shi'ite laws allow for temporary marriages, some as short as forty-eight hours. Another example is *taqiyyah* (dissimulation). If a Shi'ite living under the rule of Sunnis, were asked whether he were a Shi'ite, if he believes that answering "yes' would endanger his life, family, or property, he can morally and legally say that he is a Sunni. As for prayer, Shi'ite practice permits combining some prayers into three prayer times. A Shi'ite can often be identified by a clay tablet from a holy place on which he places his forehead while in the fully bowed position.

- Emotionalism: Shi'ite behaviour tends toward pronounced displays of inner feelings. On the Day of Ashurra male worshippers beat themselves with whips until blood flows. Holy sites such as Najaf and Karbalah along with shrines to various Shi'ite holy men are pilgrimage destinations. However, Sufi mysticism is a factor in both Sunni and Shi'ite sects.

The majority of Muslims, whether Shi'ite or Sunni, would claim that their differences do not divide them and they all remain part of the Muslim *umma*. Nevertheless, Muslim history, present politics, and age-old inter-tribal and intra-family hatreds often get in the way of harmonious relations. The word *"rafidi"* (rejector) has been used by some Sunnis to disparage Shi'ites, while Shi'ites have been known to use the term Wahabi (by Shi'ite thinking, radically un-Islamic) to negatively label Sunnis. A great political divide exists at present between Shi'ite Iran and Sunni Saudi Arabia, which may pre-date Islam as the Persians who were conquered by the Arabs, always saw their own culture as the "high culture" and the Arabs as simple "rough necks".

And now—What would you say?

FOR FURTHER DISCUSSION

THREE FAITHS—COMMON ROOT, ALMOST SIMILAR PRACTICE

The Islamic faith talks about the people of the book. These book people are the Jews, the Christians, and Muslims, and their books are the Torah, Christian Scriptures, and the Qur'an. Since all three faiths have a common scriptural ancestor, Abraham, all three faiths must have something divine at their heart. Of course Jews are descended from Abraham's second son, while Moslems are descended from Abraham's first born. And Christians follow God's son, or God incarnate, Jesus, but they stubbornly refuse to believe there was the "seal of the prophets," Mohammed, who delivered the Qur'an.

Two items need to be addressed, and both deal with the commonalities among the three faiths. The first item deals with Greek philosophy and its impact on theology. The second item deals with the similar if not identical religious practices of the three faiths. Unfortunately, in spite of these common traits, harmonious co-existence seems beyond the reach of these religions. Common roots and similar practices can as easily cause fracture and friction as they can bring about friendship and conversation.

No matter Tertullian's famous remark, "What has Athens have to do with Jerusalem?", unless we inspect Athens we will not understand three of the world's major faiths, all of which make a claim on Jerusalem. The point is that unless we begin as much with Greek philosophers Plato, Aristotle, and Zeno as we do with the Torah, we cannot get far with any discussion of common roots.

Beginning with the earliest of the three faiths, the Jewish leadership did not want anything to do with Greek thinking, so if something was going to get in, it had to sneak in. Two examples will suffice. Messianic traditions among Jews were nation-based; the nation is saved, not individual souls. Nevertheless, somewhere along the line the Pharisees began talking about resurrection of the dead. Now, rebirth and all that goes along with it is found in a series of Greek mystery religions and myths, such as those surrounding Persephone and the Eleusinian mysteries, or Bacchus/Dionysus, or Orphic practices. Plato speaks to life after death and transmigration of souls, an idea he may have picked up from a philosophic monastic group, the Pythagoreans, who operated in southern Italy.

One Jewish philosopher who wanted to meld Jewish scripture with the best philosophic thinking of his day, which was the first century B.C.E., offered that God was actually a triad composed of God, Sophia, and Shekinah. This is an interesting case because the rabbis of the time would not accept or even entertain Philo Judeaus' ideas, though Philo's writings had a great effect on early Christians.

So for the most part, Judaism until the High Middle Ages remained focused on building a clear code of ethical behavior that could be expressed both toward fellow men and women and in one's personal relation to an absolutely unitary divinity.

Jesus' disciples and apostles did not get very far with the Jews of the period, so Paul and others turned their attention to non-Jewish Greeks, Romans, Syrians, and Egyptians. On encountering the Egyptians, Christianity encountered four thousand years of magic, mystery, and a triad of gods headed up by Isis, Osiris, and Horus. On meeting the Romans, they discovered the Capitoline triad of Jupiter, Juno, and Minerva.

As Christianity moved into such centers of higher learning as Alexandria and Athens, it met with worldly philosophers who were adding to libraries scroll upon scroll of physical science, natural history, metaphysics, logic, and ethics. These philosophers were trying to understand reality from the alpha to the omega, and if they were at loggerheads with each other about almost everything, they were pretty well certain that polytheism was inane, God was one, and that there were three features of reality that had to be accounted for if any piece of philosophic speculation was to be considered wisdom.

Plato, his vision impaired by looking through a glass darkly, failed to make out that what were possible was not philosopher-kings, but philosopher-bishops, and that is the legacy of early Christianity's meeting with Greek culture and learning. Many of the bishops of the Patristic Period were trained in the good non-Christian schools, and they read not only Virgil, Ovid, and Horace, but also Plato, Aristotle, Zeno, Epicurus, and Plotinus. And for all the ranting and raving these bishops hurled at Greek learning, it is they who imported it into early medieval Christianity.

Since the Muslim world had the writings of Aristotle and Plato (the Byzantine-Roman Emperor Justinian had kicked out pagan philosophers in 529 and they went to Persia), it was not long before Muslim scientists and intellectuals sprang up and were taking shots at both the natural and supernatural world. And with the close contact of Muslims and Jews, Jewish intellectuals soon absorbed Platonic and Aristotelian thinking.

Given this dispersion of philosophic thinking, what sort of world view did these three faith share? Well, they believed the world was hierarchically structured from a basic substance at the bottom, to recognizable elements like water and earth, to plants, than animals, then humans, then angels, and at the absolute top God. They got this from Aristotle. From Plato and Aristotle they got that the Earth was in the center of the cosmos and everything in the cosmos had been made, organized, and enlivened by God. From other Greek philosophers they learned that body was bad, soul good, and women were evil temptresses. They believed in a soul that was impinged upon in not such good ways by a body, but at death that body was sloughed off and the soul would go to a better place. Greek philosophy had been transmuted into theology and the Medieval World Picture. So these three religions had great similarities, since they had all anchored themselves in Judeo-Christian scripture and then superimposed Greek philosophy.

–

And now to the second item, similar religious practices, which can be treated more concisely, because they are better known to most people. All three faiths have loyalty oaths, or rather, creeds; all see themselves as having a unitary godhead; all have the advocacy of peace, humility, love, in their ethical pronouncements; all have a notion of life after death; each personifies evil; each has a day of judgment; each eschews idolatry; each provides a way of showing piety to the Divinity; each has a set of rules for daily behavior; and each in some fashion erects a hierarchical leadership.

And truly unfortunately, all three faiths share a deeply rooted mutual animosity, which the innocents of the world have paid for and continue to pay. Muslims wiped out two-thirds of Medieval Christianity. Then in Spain and the Holy Lands, the Crusades gave the Muslims a real going over, one that is still not forgotten. As for the Jews, they had the misfortune of the Inquisition, all sorts of official and unofficial pogroms, and the Holocaust.

Of course, it wasn't only the Christians killing Muslims and Muslims killing Christians, and everyone killing the Jews. Roman Catholics killed Greek Orthodox, and vice versa, Protestants killed Roman Catholics, and vice versa, Almohads killed Almoravids, Shi'ites killed Sunnis, and everyone killed the Jews.

So we dare ask, is this the way that human beings who share common roots and similar religious practices are supposed to live? If history gives any clue, the answer is an ungodly, yes. But is all lost? Well, it really depends on whether we really believe that "Blessed are the Peacemakers." Hillel said, "The most divine thing a person can do is to turn an enemy into a friend."

And now—What would you say?

READERS' CIRCLE PROGRAM: LITERATURE FACING MECCA

A SURVEY OF NOVELS FROM *DAR AL ISLAM*

Listed here are the selections for a "Readers' Circle" program. Beyond classroom walls, students might want to form a monthly reading club and discuss all or a selection of the following works.

Fourteen novels have been selected, each prominent and excellent works of modern literature. Given that *Dar al Islam* stretches from the Atlantic to the Pacific across North Africa through the Middle East to Southeast Asia, authors representative of these different and differing Muslim areas have been selected. Two from each country (with the exception of Sudan and Saudi Arabia) were chosen to provide for more than one literary frame of reference.

From Egypt:

Palace Walk (Cairo Trilogy). Naguib Mahfuz. New York: Anchor Books/Doubleday, 1991. ISBN 0385264666. Nobel Prize winner Mahfuz takes his reader on a vivid walk through early twentieth century Egypt. This first volume of the *Cairo Trilogy* presents the disintegrating family life of a tyrannical, prosperous businessman, his retiring wife, and their rebellious children in post-WWI Egypt.

The Cairo House. Samia Serageldin. Syracuse, New York: Syracuse University Press, 2000. ISBN 0815607938. Serageldin writes in a semi-autobiographical fashion from the United States about life in Egypt in the 1950s, 60s, and early 70s as Egypt moved into the modern age.

From India:

Imaginary Maps: Three Stories. Mahasweta Devi. New York: Routledge, 1994. ISBN 0415904633. Mixing together myth, history, and political practicalities, Ms. Devi's writing exposes the life of the poor lower class workers of post-colonial India.

Satanic Verses. Salman Rushdie. New York: Random House Trade Paperbacks, 2008 (original date 1988). ISBN-10 0812976711. The title of this wonderful work of fiction refers to verses the devil made Mohammad speak. The book earned Rushdie a *fatwa* that proclaimed that anyone could kill him for this literary indiscretion. Rushdie is an Indian who grew up in Tinidad.

From Indonesia:

Overboard. Elizabeth Fama. Peterborough, New Hampshire: Cricket Books, 2002. ISBN 0812626524. This is a book for teenagers about a young girl who tries to survive after the ferry she is on sinks. It is based on a true story.

And the War Is Over: A Novel. Ismail Marahimin. New York: Grove Press, 2002. ISBN 0802139221. The novel is set at the end of WWII, and Marahimin reviews the personal interactions of the Dutch, Japanese, and Sumatrans in the village of Teratakbuluh. The book was the winner of the prestigious Pegasus Prize in Literature.

From Iran:

Veils: Short Stories. Nahid Rachlin. San Francisco: City Lights Books, 1992. ISBN 0872862674. Quoted *From Publishers Weekly*—"These 10 stories by Ms. Rachlin track unhappy Iranians who reside in their native country or live as expatriates in America."

Savushun: A Novel About Modern Iran. Simin Danishvar. Washington: D.C.: Mage Publishers, 1991. ISBN 0934211310. The author reviews the life of a Persian family during the Western occupation of Iran during WW II.

From the Mahgreb:

The Sand Child. Tahar Ben Jelloun (Moroccan). Baltimore: Johns Hopkins Press, 2000. ISBN 0801864402. This is a story of a man who is saddened because he has only fathered daughters, so his eighth female child he presents to the world as a male.

So Vast a Prison: a Novel. Assia Djebar (Algerian). New York: Seven Stories Press. 2001. ISBN 1583220674. In colorful and poetic language, the author describes the life of Algerian women and their faith and desires.

From Saudi Arabia:

The Tree and Other Short Stories. Abdallah Al-Nasser. Northampton, Maine: Interlink Publishing Group, 2004. ISBN 1566564980. Many of these stories explore, in often unexpected fashion, life in the author's Saudi homeland. Al-Nasser presents the traditional aspects of his culture and the effect the contemporary world has had on them.

From Sudan:

A Season of Migration to the North. Tayeb Saleh. Portsmouth, New Hampshire: Heinemann Publishers, 1970. ISBN 0435900668. Quoted *From Publishers Weekly*— "One of the classic themes followed in this complex novel, translated from the Arabic, is cultural dissonance between East and West, particularly the experience of a returned native. The narrator returns from his studies in England to his remote little village in Sudan, to begin his career as an educator. There he encounters the mysterious Mustafa."

From Turkey:

The White Castle. Orhan Pamuk. New York: Vintage Books, 1998. ISBN 0375701613. One of Turkey's foremost novelists, Pamuk writes surreal novels that focus on aspects of medieval Moslem culture.

Iron Earth Copper Sky. Yashar Kemal. New York: HarperCollins,1992. ASIN 0002713500. A master story-teller, Kemal presents Anatolian myths as convincing as facts to urban populations.

RESOURCE BIBLIOGRAPHY

The materials listed here are suggestions for classroom texts and general resource books for a semester-long introductory course to Islam. So many books on Muslims and the Islamic faith have been published in the last twenty years, it is impossible to keep up with them. The same can be said for internet sites—some trustworthy other *diaif*.

Possible classroom textbooks:

Armstrong, Karen. *Islam: A Short History.* New York: Modern Library, Random House, 2002.

Cook, Michael. *The Koran: A Very Short Introduction.* New York: Oxford University Press, 2000.

Esposito, John. *What Everyone Needs to Know About Islam.* New York: Oxford University Press, 2002.

Lewis, Bernard. *Islam and the West.* New York: Oxford University Press, 1993.

Lewis, Bernard, and Churchill, Buntzie Ellis. *Islam: The Religion and the People.* Upper Saddle River, New Jersey: Pearson Education, Inc., 2009.

Lings, Martin. *Mohammed: His Life Based on the Earliest Sources.* Rochester, Vermont: Inner Traditions. Revised edition, 2006.

Peters, F.E., *A Reader on Classical Islam.* Princeton, New Jersey: Princeton University Press, 1993.

Selected Qur'ans:

Qur'an, The. Oxford World Classics. M.A.S. Abdel Haleem., translator. New York: Oxford University Press (reissue), 2008.

The Meaning of the Holy Qur'an, by Abdullah Yusuf Ali. Amana Publications.

Saheeh International Qur'an (www.saheehinternational.com/qurantranslation).

Resource books:

Ansary, Mir Tamim. *Destiny Disrupted: A History of the World Through Islamic Eyes.* New York: Public Affairs. Reprint edition, 2010.

Azlan, Reza. *No God but God: The Origins, Evolution, and Future of Islam.* New York: Random House Trade Paperbacks, 2006.

Cambridge Companion to the Qur'an, The. (Cambridge Companions to Religion). Jane McAuliffe, editor. Cambridge, United Kingdom: Cambridge University Press, 2006.

Cambridge Illustrated History of the Islamic World. Edward Robinson, editor. Cambridge, United Kingdom: Cambridge University Press, 1999.

Esposito, John. *Oxford History of Islam*. New York: Oxford University Press, 2000.

Grunebaum, G.E. von. *Classical Islam. A History 600 to 1258*. New York: Barnes Noble Books. 1997.

Guillaume, Alfred. The Life of Mohammed. Oxford: Oxford University Press, 1955.

Hitti, Philip. *History of the Arabs, Revised: 10ᵗʰ Edition*. New York: Palgrave MacMillan, 2002.

Hourani, Albert. *A History of the Arab People*. New York: Warner Books, 1992

Islam and the Arab World: Faith. People. Culture. Bernard Lewis, editor. New York: Alfred A. Knopf. 1976.

Islam Art and Culture. Markus Hattstein and Peter Delius, editors.New York: Konemann. 2004.

Nasr, Seyyed. *Islam: Religion, History, Civilization*. New York: Harper One. 2002.

Ruthven, Malise. *Islam in the World*. Third edition. New York: Oxford Press, 2006.

Treasures of Islam. Toby Falk, editor. Edison, New Jersey: Wellfleet Press. 1985.

SAMPLE TEST QUESTIONS

This sampling of test questions is for a semester-long course, meeting once a week for fifteen sessions, each session being two and a half hours.

SAMPLE TEST QUESTIONS 1:

Instructions for in-class six-question test: In essay fashion respond to any three of the following six questions. Write a complete and detailed well-formed essay. Each fully correct response (extent of content, comprehension, presentation) is worth 33.3 points.

      Instructions for take-home six-question test: In essay fashion respond to any three of the following six questions. Write at least 1000 words and no more than 1200 words for each well-formed essay (three to four typed pages—cite word count). Please underline the required terms. Each fully correct response (extent of content, comprehension, presentation—grammar, punctuation, syntax, spelling) is worth 33.3 points.

1.   What are the five core beliefs that unite all Muslims? Explain them in detail. What do Muslims believe about Allah? What do Muslims believe about Mohammad?

2.   Why might one call the period from the 8th to the 13th centuries the Golden Age of Islam? How did Islamic "governments" and societies operate in the earliest years? What causes could be cited for the supposed decline of *Dar al Islam* as a "light" and "force" in the world.

3.   In what ways did Greek philosophy influence Islamic philosophy? Examine the conflict between the Mu'tazilites and Ash'arites. Examine the philosophy of Avicenna and Averroes. How did al Ghazzali put a "damper" on rationalist philosophical-scientific thinking?

4.   Present historical information surrounding the birth of Islam. Can you cite some pre-Islamic ideas or ideas from other religions and show how Islam has adopted or adapted these? What was the Age of Jahiliya (confusion)? What were Mecca and Arabia like?

5.   What is the foundation(s) of Islamic law? Can you summarize how an Islamic law court works? What is the purpose of a *isnad*? What is the purpose of a *fatwa*? Could applying Islamic law successfully run a modern society? What would be its benefits? Its shortcomings?

6.   What is a theocracy? Can the term be successfully applied to early *Dar al-Islam*, later Islamic empires, today's Islamicate countries, or is it an altogether misleading application of the term? What observations (regarding *salafiism*, etc.) could be made about Islam as a religious and political force in the 20th and 21st century in various countries?

7. Beginning with the Treaty of Carlowicz 1699, discuss the modern development of Western nations and the effects modern Western nations have had on *Dar al Islam*. Consider in your response the idea of theocracy. Can the term be successfully applied to early *Dar al Islam*, later empires, today's Muslim countries, or is it an altogether misleading application of the term?

8. What is the foundation(s) of Islamic *fiqh*—the various means/tools by which it is derived? Can you summarize how an Islamic law court works? What is the purpose of a *fatwa*? Discuss women's rights (or the lack thereof) under Islamic law.

9. Describe the Qur'an. How is it structured? How is it related to Christianity? What moral principles are found in the book and by extension how *shari'a* (along with hadith and sunna) is developed from it.

10. Scholars wonder if much pre-Islamic material—ethical codes and ideas about life and divinity—got adopted into the Qur'an and Islamic tradition. Detail how Mohammad affects this historical setting.

SAMPLE TEST QUESTIONS 2:

Instructions for in-class six-question test: In essay fashion respond to any three of the following six listings. Write a complete and detailed well-formed essay. Each fully correct response (extent of content, comprehension, presentation) is worth 33.3 points.

Instructions for take-home six-question test: In essay fashion respond to any three of the following six listings. Write at least 1000 words and no more than 1200 words for each well-formed essay (three to four typed pages—cite word count). Please underline the required terms. Each fully correct response (extent of content, comprehension, presentation—grammar, punctuation, syntax, spelling) is worth 33.3 points.

Essay A:

1. Khadija; 2. ghazi; 3. hijira; 4. Aisha; 5. rashidun; 6. Sunni; 7. Shi'ite; 8. Fatima; 9. baraq; 10. Gabriel.

Essay B:

1. Mecca; 2. Medina; 3. Battle of Badr; 4. Kaaba; 5. Dome of the Rock;

6. Constantinople; 7. Battle of Manzikurt; 8. Reconquista; 9. Crusades; 10. Mamluks.

Essay C:

1. Shari'a; 2. hadith; 3. sunna; 4. fatwa; 5. taqlid; 6. qiyas; 7. ijtihad; 8. mufti; 9. qadi; 10. fiqh.

Essay D:

1. Five Pillars; 2. shahada; 3. zakat; 4. salat; 5. sura; 6. Koran/Quran; 7. sawm; 8. hajj; 9. Muslim; 10. ridda.

Essay E:

1. Mongol Invasions; 2. Treaty of Carlowicz; 3. Mughal Empire; 4. Safavid Empire; 5. Ottoman Empire; 6. Ikhwan al Muslimun; 7. Wahabism; 8. Taliban; 9. Al Qaeda; 10. jihad.

Essay F:

1. Bayt al Hikma; 2. Mu'tazilites; 3. Ash'arites; 4. Al Kindi; 5. Ibn Sina (Avicenna); 6. Al Ghazzali; 7. Sufism; 8. creation (of world); 9. Sir Sayyid Ahmad Khan; 10. Sayyid Qutb.